Strategic Brand Management In and Through Sport

This book explores how sport brands can be managed strategically, as well as how non-sport brands can be managed strategically through their association with sport.

Despite decades of extensive research, brand management remains a priority for academics and practitioners alike. To this day, ample new and insightful research is being conducted on the matter, with questions around how a brand can be managed strategically still emerging. As the knowledge on the issue deepens, so does our interest in fully comprehending the fascinating and ever-developing strategic brand management, bearing in mind the ever-shifting environment in which brands operate.

A particularly interesting topic within the wider brand management literature is brand management both in and through sport. The study of how sport brands can be managed strategically, as well as how non-sport brands can be managed strategically through their association with sport remains an interesting and unique field, offering valuable insights due to sport's natural marketing advantage caused by people's increased interest in sport and its socio-cultural importance in our lives.

This book explores strategic brand management both in and through sport, thus helping in deepening our understanding of this promising field, while offering directions for future research in the area. The chapters in this book were originally published in the *Journal of Strategic Marketing*.

Argyro Elisavet Manoli is Associate Professor of Marketing and Management in University of Bergamo. Following a career as a sports marketeer, Prof. Manoli began her academic career in the UK. Her research interests focus on two broad areas, marketing communications management and integrity management in the context of sport.

Strategic Brand Management In and Through Sport

Edited by
Argyro Elisavet Manoli

LONDON AND NEW YORK

First published 2025
by Routledge
4 Park Square, Milton Park, Abingdon, Oxon OX14 4RN

and by Routledge
605 Third Avenue, New York, NY 10158

Routledge is an imprint of the Taylor & Francis Group, an informa business

Preface © 2025 Argyro Elisavet Manoli.
Chapters 2–4, 6 and 7 © 2025 Taylor & Francis.
Chapter 1 © 2022 Argyro Elisavet Manoli. Originally published as Open Access.
Chapter 5 © 2021 Robin Ireland, Magdalena Muc, Christopher Bunn & Emma Boyland. Originally published as Open Access.

With the exception of Chapters 1 and 5, no part of this book may be reprinted or reproduced or utilised in any form or by any electronic, mechanical, or other means, now known or hereafter invented, including photocopying and recording, or in any information storage or retrieval system, without permission in writing from the publishers. For details on the rights for Chapters 1 and 5, please see the chapters' Open Access footnotes.

Trademark notice: Product or corporate names may be trademarks or registered trademarks, and are used only for identification and explanation without intent to infringe.

British Library Cataloguing in Publication Data
A catalogue record for this book is available from the British Library

ISBN13: 978-1-032-96827-8 (hbk)
ISBN13: 978-1-032-96829-2 (pbk)
ISBN13: 978-1-003-59085-9 (ebk)

DOI: 10.4324/9781003590859

Typeset in Myriad Pro
by Newgen Publishing UK

Publisher's Note
The publisher accepts responsibility for any inconsistencies that may have arisen during the conversion of this book from journal articles to book chapters, namely the inclusion of journal terminology.

Disclaimer
Every effort has been made to contact copyright holders for their permission to reprint material in this book. The publishers would be grateful to hear from any copyright holder who is not here acknowledged and will undertake to rectify any errors or omissions in future editions of this book.

Contents

	Citation Information	vii
	Notes on Contributors	ix
	Preface	x
	Argyro Elisavet Manoli	
1	Strategic brand management in and through sport Argyro Elisavet Manoli	1
2	Seeing the same things differently: exploring the unique brand associations linked to women's professional sport teams Jason Patrick Doyle, Thilo Kunkel, Sarah Jane Kelly, Kevin Filo and Graham Cuskelly	9
3	Building team brand equity through perceived CSR: the mediating role of dual identification Sungkyung Kim and Argyro Elisavet Manoli	24
4	Strategic sport marketing in the society of the spectacle André Richelieu and Andrew Webb	39
5	Marketing of unhealthy brands during the 2018 Fédération Internationale de Football Association (FIFA) World Cup UK broadcasts – a frequency analysis Robin Ireland, Magdalena Muc, Christopher Bunn and Emma Boyland	57
6	Strategic marketing through sport for development: managing multi-stakeholder partnerships Andrew Webb and Krystn Orr	73

7 Does team identification of satellite fans influence brand-related sponsorship outcomes? What we learned from Manchester United supporters in Malaysia 90
Charitomeni Tsordia, Artemisia Apostolopoulou and Dimitra Papadimitriou

Index 109

Citation Information

The following chapters in this book were originally published in the *Journal of Strategic Marketing*, volume 32, issue 6 (2024), except Chapter 3, which was published in volume 30, issue 3 (2022). When citing this material, please use the original page numbering for each article, as follows:

Chapter 1
Strategic brand management in and through sport
Argyro Elisavet Manoli
Journal of Strategic Marketing, volume 32, issue 6 (2024), pp. 814–821

Chapter 2
Seeing the same things differently: exploring the unique brand associations linked to women's professional sport teams
Jason Patrick Doyle, Thilo Kunkel, Sarah Jane Kelly, Kevin Filo and Graham Cuskelly
Journal of Strategic Marketing, volume 32, issue 6 (2024), pp. 729–743

Chapter 3
Building team brand equity through perceived CSR: the mediating role of dual identification
Sungkyung Kim and Argyro Elisavet Manoli
Journal of Strategic Marketing, volume 30, issue 3 (2022), pp. 281–295

Chapter 4
Strategic sport marketing in the society of the spectacle
André Richelieu and Andrew Webb
Journal of Strategic Marketing, volume 32, issue 6 (2024), pp. 744–761

Chapter 5
Marketing of unhealthy brands during the 2018 Fédération Internationale de Football Association (FIFA) World Cup UK broadcasts – a frequency analysis
Robin Ireland, Magdalena Muc, Christopher Bunn and Emma Boyland
Journal of Strategic Marketing, volume 32, issue 6 (2024), pp. 762–777

Chapter 6
Strategic marketing through sport for development: managing multi-stakeholder partnerships
Andrew Webb and Krystn Orr
Journal of Strategic Marketing, volume 32, issue 6 (2024), pp. 778–794

Chapter 7
Does team identification of satellite fans influence brand-related sponsorship outcomes? What we learned from Manchester United supporters in Malaysia
Charitomeni Tsordia, Artemisia Apostolopoulou and Dimitra Papadimitriou
Journal of Strategic Marketing, volume 32, issue 6 (2024), pp. 795–813

For any permission-related enquiries please visit:
www.tandfonline.com/page/help/permissions

Notes on Contributors

Artemisia Apostolopoulou, Departments of Sport Management and Marketing, Robert Morris University, Moon Township, PA, USA.

Emma Boyland, Department of Psychology, University of Liverpool, UK.

Christopher Bunn, School of Social and Political Sciences, University of Glasgow, UK.

Graham Cuskelly, Department of Tourism, Sport, and Hotel Management, Griffith Business School, Griffith University, Queensland, Australia.

Jason Patrick Doyle, Department of Tourism, Sport, and Hotel Management, Griffith Business School, Griffith University, Queensland, Australia.

Kevin Filo, Department of Tourism, Sport, and Hotel Management, Griffith Business School, Griffith University, Queensland, Australia.

Robin Ireland, School of Social and Political Sciences, University of Glasgow, UK.

Sarah Jane Kelly, Faculty of Business, Economics and Law, School of Business, The University of Queensland, Brisbane, Queensland, Australia.

Sungkyung Kim, School of Sport, Exercise and Health Sciences, Loughborough University, Loughborough, UK.

Thilo Kunkel, School of Sport, Tourism, and Hospitality Management, Temple University, Philadelphia, PA, USA.

Argyro Elisavet Manoli, Department of Management, University of Bergamo, Italy.

Magdalena Muc, Department of Psychology, University of Liverpool, UK.

Krystn Orr, School of Social Work, McMaster University, Hamilton, Canada.

Dimitra Papadimitriou, Department of Business Administration, University of Patras, Patras, Greece.

André Richelieu, Consultant & Expert in 'Sportainment'; Marketing Department, ESG UQAM, Montreal, Canada.

Charitomeni Tsordia, Department of Business Administration, University of Patras, Patras, Greece.

Andrew Webb, Sprott School of Business, Carleton University, Ottawa, Canada.

Preface

Argyro Elisavet Manoli

In today's highly competitive global marketplace, brand management has become a central component of business success across industries, but few sectors offer the unique branding opportunities and challenges that sport does. The sports arena is not just a stage for athletes to compete; it is a dynamic platform for building and managing powerful brands that resonate deeply with millions, if not billions, of people around the world.

Sport is more than just entertainment. It is a source of passion, identity, and community for fans, creating a level of emotional engagement that few other industries can replicate. The loyalty of sports fans is not fleeting—it is deeply rooted in tradition, personal identity, and shared experiences. As a result, brands associated with sport, whether they are leagues, teams, individual athletes, or commercial partners, must navigate this emotional landscape carefully to build lasting and authentic relationships with their audiences.

This book, *Strategic Brand Management In and Through Sport*, was born out of a desire to explore the distinct intersection of sport and brand management. While branding concepts like identity, equity, and positioning apply universally, the sports world operates with its own unique dynamics. The intense emotional connections fans have with teams and athletes, the global visibility of major sporting events, and the digital revolution transforming fan engagement all present both opportunities and challenges for those looking to build strong brands in this space.

Purpose and Scope

The purpose of this book is to provide a comprehensive understanding of how brand management functions within the world of sport. It is intended for sports marketers, brand managers, and students of sports management, as well as anyone interested in understanding how sports can serve as a powerful branding tool.

Through real-world examples, we will explore the core elements of strategic brand management, including brand identity, equity building, athlete branding, sponsorship strategies, and the pivotal role of corporate social responsibility and brand experiences in modern fan engagement. We will also examine the unique challenges sports brands face, from managing reputational risks to ensuring sustained fan loyalty in an ever-evolving global and digital age.

This book is designed to serve not only academics and professionals directly involved in sports, but also those outside the industry looking to leverage the universal appeal and emotional power of sport to enhance their own brands. From corporations sponsoring sporting events to athletes becoming individual brands in their own right, the lessons in this book can be applied across diverse fields.

Why Now?

The landscape of sport is undergoing a profound transformation. The rise of digital media has reshaped how fans engage with their favourite teams and athletes, making social platforms integral to brand strategies. Athletes have become brands themselves, cultivating direct connections with millions of followers across the globe. Meanwhile, brands looking to attach themselves to the passion of sport must navigate increasingly complex environments to ensure their messages are authentic and relevant.

At the same time, the globalization of sport has expanded the market for brands, making it possible for teams and athletes to build followings across continents. This new reality presents incredible opportunities, but also the challenge of appealing to culturally diverse and dispersed audiences.

As the sports world continues to evolve, mastering strategic brand management is critical for anyone looking to thrive in this space. This book aims to provide you with the tools and insights necessary to truly appreciate this landscape, whether you are focusing on managing a sports brand or using sport as a vehicle to enhance a broader brand.

My Motivation

Having spent years working and studying the fields of sports marketing and brand management, I have witnessed first-hand the profound impact that a well-executed brand strategy can have on both an organization and its audience. The relationship between sport and branding is not just a professional interest for me—it is a passion. Whether it is a football team with a century of history or a young athlete using social media to build a personal brand, the dynamics at play in sports branding are endlessly fascinating, and I wanted to bring this knowledge together in a form that would be accessible and useful to professionals and students alike.

Structure of the Book

The book is divided into two key sections. We begin with the examination of strategic brand management in sport, by focusing on athletes and sport organizations that are integral parts of the sport ecosystem. From there, we delve into the exploration of how sport is and can be used as a tool for strategic brand management for non-sport organizations, such as healthy and unhealthy brands, as well as sport for development programmes. Throughout, we will examine real-world case studies to illustrate how successful brands have navigated these waters, as well as cautionary tales where things might deviate from the intended outcome.

Acknowledgements

I would like to extend my deepest thanks to the authors of the chapters of this book who contributed their much-needed research on the topic, offering valuable lessons in the art and science of strategic brand management. I would like to also thank the participants of their studies, as well as their supporting institutions and of course Routledge for providing the required assistance in order for this book to come to life.

Call to Action

As you explore the chapters ahead, I encourage you to think about the ways in which sport can be leveraged to create stronger, more emotionally resonant brands. Whether you are studying how to or indeed building yourself a sports brand from the ground up or using sport as a tool to connect with your audience, the strategies and insights shared here can help you navigate this exciting and challenging field.

Strategic brand management in sport is not just about logos and slogans; it is about understanding and harnessing the power of passion, loyalty, and identity. I hope this book equips you with the knowledge and tools to study and build brands that not only stand the test of time but also connect with people on a deeper level.

Strategic brand management in and through sport

Argyro Elisavet Manoli

ABSTRACT
Within the extended academic literature on strategic marketing, brand management appears to be high on the agenda of scholars in the past seven decades. Despite the continuous enquiry over these years, the way in which a brand can or should be managed in a strategic manner appears to still attract academics' and practitioners' interest, with novel and often unexpected ideas and practices emerging. Among these, brand management within sport and through it remains a unique area for further enquiry, and one that is bound to yield interesting insights due to the social, political, geographical, cultural, and historical peculiarities of sport, granting it a natural 'marketing' advantage. This article explores the evolution of brand management, its manifestation in and through sport, and its potential future directions within and beyond the ever-developing sport ecosystem.

Introduction

The topic of brand management has attracted remarkable attention within academia throughout the past seven decades, with numerous scholars attempting to define, explore, and even reconceptualise what a brand is, how it is developed, how it is perceived, and ultimately how it can be managed (Aaker, 1989; Fulmer, 1965; Keller, 1993). Within these seven decades, attitudes and paradigms have shifted; debates have been created, analysed, and sometimes abandoned; schools of thought have been formed; and questions have been asked, answered, and sometimes re-formed and re-emerged, with one thing remaining unchanged: brand management has yet to run its course in academia. Among the various forms and shapes brand management can take, brand management in sport or through sport appears to attract increasing interest by both academia and practice (Bauer et al., 2005; Gladden & Funk, 2001; Richelieu, 2016). This introduction to the special issue of Strategic Brand Management In and Through Sport discusses how brand management has evolved over time, how it materialises in and through sport, as well as the shapes it can be expected to take in the future.

Brand management over time

In the early discussions focusing on a brand and its management, the former was often perceived to be a rather rigid instrument value, created by an organisation and managed strictly by them, or more precisely by the 'brand-man' within each company as Fulmer put it (Fulmer, 1965, p. 65). The brand at that point was often viewed as an additional asset a company held, which was of some, undefined value, that was nevertheless part of a company's strategic portfolio.

With similar ideas persisting for a few decades (Lear, 1963), it was not until the late '80s and '90s that the strategic value of a brand was brought to the forefront for analysis (Aaker, 1989). The discussions emerging at that point presented the brand as a key asset to an organisation, assisting it in acquiring a competitive advantage over its competition. At the same time, it was also suggested that the brand's value was intrinsically associated not only with the way in which a brand was formed and managed but also most importantly with the way in which it was perceived (Aaker, 1991; Keller, 1993). It is the ability of the brand to bring this competitive advantage that emphasised its strategic value and therefore the importance of its management to an organisation. Around this time, the pivotal research of two scholars, David Aaker and Kevin Lane Keller, set the foundations of our modern-day understanding of a brand and its components. In fact, it is worth noting that their work – dating back to the 1990s – is still being quoted and used in brand management research worldwide as the starting point of reconceptualising and dissecting a brand to the various elements it comprises. The brand at that point in time was beginning to be perceived as more consumer focused; putting the spotlight on the customer rather than the brand manager, diverging from previous research (Aaker, 1991, 1997; Keller, 1993, 2003). That new perspective unlocked an array of new concepts and vocabulary through studies that addressed topics such as brand identity, brand meaning, brand response, brand relationships, brand awareness, brand associations, perceived quality, brand loyalty, and brand equity. One could argue that these terms, the frameworks in which they were being introduced, and the way in which they captured how a brand is perceived as a strategic asset for an organisation, marked the beginning of the reconceptualisation of brand management. It was a catalyst for change, as forwarding thinking organisations recognised the value of dramatically broadening the purview of brand management. It was no longer simply a marketing function with strategic value, but a strategic management function with significant potential to influence the profitability and success of an organisation (Harris & de Chernatony, 2001).

Studies conducted in the 2000s have further emphasised the strategic value of brand management by once again rethinking how the brand is created and who should be considered the key target group of a brand. At that point, the appreciation of brand management progressed from being considered a linear paradigm or a monologue from a brand to its customers, to an interactive paradigm or a dialogue between a brand and its audience. Research at that time highlights the flexible nature of the brand, which is attributed to the way in which it is co-created among all relevant stakeholders, who are no longer limited to the customers (or prospective customers) and the employees of an organisation (Pongsakornrungsilp & Schroeder, 2011; Zhang et al., 2015). Instead, a wider realm of stakeholders is being considered, broadening our understanding of what a brand represents, and further expanding the nature of brand management. According to these recent studies, brand management is no longer confined to simply managing a brand but expands to managing people, processes, channels, and results connected with a brand, further emphasising the repositioning of brand management as a strategic management function (Keller, 2016; Manoli, 2020). It is within these studies that the idea of strategic brand management is linked with another emerging area of study and practice, integrating marketing communications *throughout* an organisation and *over time* (Luxton et al., 2017; Manoli & Hodgkinson, 2020).

As the above discussion has illustrated, interestingly, after almost seven decades of analysis and exploration, we find ourselves still asking questions about how to better understand a brand, its value, its development, and its management. Questions that are further emphasised by new enquiries on brand consistency, or inconsistency, among different stakeholders, stakeholder overlap, traditional and digital medial proliferation, and power shifts from the organisation to the stakeholders (Harris & de Chernatony, 2001; Kenyon et al., 2018; Manoli & Hodgkinson, 2020) as well as the strategic managerial implications that arise from these issues. It is in fact within these strategic implications, both theoretically and managerially, that this special issue aims its focus, while concentrating on the exciting and ever-evolving sector of sport.

Sport is now considered one of the most quickly and steadily developing sectors worldwide, with growth noted amidst numerous national and international crises. As a result, sport has and still is attracting remarkable attention from scholars and practitioners alike, as a previous special issue in this journal illustrated (see Manoli, 2018). Sport brands, their unique characteristics, audience generated importance, and subsequent emotional attachment have been capturing significant interest, not only within academia but also within practitioners who have been exploring ways in which to develop and manage brands, both in and through sport (Bauer et al., 2005; Henseler et al., 2011; Richelieu, 2016). As a consequence, strategic brand management in this special issue is examined through two lenses: strategic brand management in sport (i.e. within the sector) and strategic brand management through sport (i.e. with sport used as a platform for the strategic management of other brands). More specifically, this special issue – comprising six selected peer-reviewed articles – aims to enrich the ever-developing branding and sport branding literature, by exploring some of the forms that strategic sport brand management can take while bearing in mind its strategic nature, the rapid development of the sport sector, and the wider social, technological, and financial environment.

Strategic brand management in sport

As is often argued in management practices within the sport ecosystem, the modern sport industry developed at an extremely fast pace, reacting to the increased interest it received from various stakeholders, such as the public and the media, as well as from other corporate partners (Manoli & Hodgkinson, 2017; McCarthy et al., 2014). Following this rapid increase in interest – and paired with the wider pressures brought over by the commercialisation, commodification, and globalisation of the broader environment – the sport industry was called to develop almost overnight, reacting to the demand and not pro-actively planning for it. As such, appropriate procedures and protocols were often found to poorly implemented or even entirely absent. However, and despite these original challenges, the uniqueness of sport and most importantly the efforts of the individuals employed within it have allowed the sector to develop its strategic marketing practices to an arguably highly advanced state. It is in fact these unique characteristics that have set sport apart in terms of brand management (Gladden & Funk, 2001).

Sport has the power to evoke strong emotions in its fans (customers), which is a key ingredient in building their loyalty. In brand management terms, this would translate to a very high brand loyalty, in which any switching costs are too high for a customer to consider any other competitor brand (Fawbert, 2017). This high identification with a brand can often be considered rather unique to sport, especially when compared to consumer brands who might struggle to achieve lower levels of loyalty, based on quality or price differentiation. At the same time, the social, political, geographical, cultural, and historical aspects and associations incorporated and surrounding sport give it a natural 'marketing advantage' as Manoli and Kenyon (2018, p. 89) argue in terms of building brand equity. This in turn makes strategic brand management in sport rather unique and, as a previous special issue in this journal illustrated (see Manoli, 2018), a fascinating area of study.

The ample existing literature on brand management in sport has provided extant analysis on remarkable practices in both applying 'traditional' brand management practices in sport and creating unique approaches to building sport brands and extending them. The following three articles included in this special issue shed further light on such practices adopted within the sport sector, further enriching our understanding of strategic brand management in sport.

The first article by Doyle et al. (2021) examines brand associations in the quickly developing women's sport. Using brand architecture and brand association knowledge, their work explores the perceptions of consumers of women's professional sports team brands in Australia. Interestingly, as their study argues, historical, economic, and societal conditions or pre-dispositions influence consumers' perceptions both positively and negatively, with the latter appearing to be unique in women's professional sports teams' brands. In terms of the former, positive associations, the study offers insights to distinctive favourable associations, which help highlight opportunities for how strategic brand management in sport (of the teams) and through sport (of the teams' associated stakeholders, e.g. sponsors) can further develop.

In the second article of this special issue, Kim and Manoli (2020) focus on strategic brand management in sport, and in particular the mechanism through which a sport team's brand equity can be built through customers' (fans') perceptions of the team's corporate social responsibility. Their study centres on a South Korean baseball club and adds the additional layer of fans' identification, both with their team and with an online community of which they are members, in order to further explore its influence on brand equity. Through this exploration, it is argued that a team's socially responsible image cannot by itself result in building brand equity, despite its importance in building fans' identification. This suggests that fans' identification and the use of online communities might be the key to strategic brand management in sport.

In the third article of this special issue, by Richelieu and Webb (2021), the creation of 'sportainment' is discussed as the result of the merger of sport and entertainment, as seen through the lens of the society of the spectacle where entertainment is made the focal point of any experience. By focusing on a polar or extreme case study, their research introduces a strategic sportainment mix which encapsulates how strategic marketing and brand management, both in and through sport, can adapt to better respond to the needs and opportunities of the current era and the modern consumer of sport. The proposed sportainment mix can then assist in increasing both the value of the sport consumer and the customer- and financial-based brand equity of the organisations involved.

Strategic brand management through sport

As it has been argued over the past two decades, a number of relatively new challenges exist for modern strategic marketing. The multiplication of media and the rapid growth of social media, paired with their often remarkably quick popularity and short life expectancy, have resulted in a dramatic increase in messages and information offering, leading to what we can call marketing 'noise' for the consumers (Schultz et al., 2013). This endless stream of information, coming in many forms and sizes, from text and images to videos and interactive content, landing directly into people's pockets, hands, and eyes, appear to be 'bombarding' consumers. This increasing 'noise' in the eyes and ears of the consumer has resulted in audiences becoming better accustomed to filtering and often simply ignoring information presented directly to them and has spurred a new more challenging era for marketing, the era of permission marketing (Tezinde et al., 2002). In this era, as it is argued, brands have to request the audience's permission and win their attention in order for their messages to be heard and seen. As a result, an additional effort or sometimes struggle is required from brands to attract (potential and existing) customers, win (or 'fight' to win) their attention, and promote their message in a way that could resonate with them.

It is because of this increasing difficulty, and the corresponding struggle, that some brands have re-focused their brand management efforts on differentiating themselves in the eyes of the consumer; through the promotion of their brands' unique characteristics (Ehrenberg et al., 1997). In this effort to build or re-shape their brand image to something more unique, non-sport-related brands have often found sport to be the ideal vehicle. Sport, with its unique brands, high brand awareness, remarkable brand identification, emotional attachment, and strong sociological, cultural, and historic brand associations (as discussed above), becomes a platform on which a non-sport-related brand can build their strategic brand management in order to differentiate themselves from their competitors. Therefore, strategic brand management through sport encapsulates a number of activities through which a non-sport-related brand associates themselves with sport in order to gain memorability and uniqueness in the eyes of the consumers and consequently gain a competitive advantage in today's challenging marketplace.

The following three articles in this special issue explore this practice further, offering valuable insights on strategic brand management through sport.

The fourth article in this special issue by Ireland et al. (2021) explores the topical issue of unhealthy brand promotion through sport, by examining the marketing references and exposure of brands of (what are perceived to be) unhealthy products in the live broadcast of the 2018 FIFA Men's World Cup tournament on UK television. By focusing on the contemporary topic of unhealthy products and their promotion, the study offers details on the wider strategic, ethical, and societal implications of brand management through sport (for example through sponsorship and advertising). It also highlights that the strategic and monetary value of brand management through sport can act as indicators of the globalisation and commodification of sport in today's world, offering a different conceptual understanding of the present and future of strategic sport marketing.

In the fifth article, Webb and Orr (2021) focus on strategic brand management through sport for development, linking the ever-evolving area of strategic marketing through sport with corporate social responsibility. By exploring how non-sport-related organisations partner with other stakeholders in order to improve the lives of individuals identifying with intellectual disabilities through sport, this study sheds light on an interesting and challenging practice which has received little attention within the marketing literature. Their research enhances our conceptual understanding of how corporate partners can be activated in such a multi-stakeholder partnership, in order to further develop their brand value and achieve their strategic brand management objectives through sport.

The final article of this special issue by Tsordia et al. (2021) focuses on brand management through sport, by exploring the lessons that can be learned from the outcomes of sport teams' sponsorships on satellite fans, who are the fans (customers) of a sport team that are not local to the area in which the team is based. The study examines how fans of Manchester United FC who are based in Malaysia perceive the sponsor of the club, shedding light on the wider brand management effects for non-sporting companies who opt to strategically engage with sport team sponsorship to manage their brand, while similar studies exploring the effects on a sponsor's perceived brand quality and word-of-mouth deriving from their decision to sponsor a sport team have been conducted on local fans examining that satellite fans allows this study to highlight the wider, global effects, of such a decision, further emphasising the value of strategic brand management through sport.

The future of strategic brand management in and through sport

While it needs to be highlighted that this special issue by no means exhausts the ever-developing issue of brand management in and through sport, the articles included within it offer novel and valuable insights in the area. The articles included in this special issue address the topic from diverse viewpoints, contributing to our conceptual understanding of the subject that can help better pave the way for both future research and practice, both on and in, the area. While the sport ecosystem is bound to keep developing in potentially unexpected or unpredictable ways, being driven forward by both its international growth and the external pressures and opportunities with which it is faced, new practices and trends in regard to strategic brand management in and through sport are also expected to emerge. We can safely assume that these will involve the development and further utilisation of evolving sport, such as women's sport, e-sport, and new or alternative sport, as areas to advance or platforms to help advance the strategic brand management within and beyond sport. In addition, existing popular practices in the area, such as commercial partnerships between sport and non-sport-related organisations, are bound to be further explored and 'exploited' in the coming years, while incorporating new elements emerging from the environment in which the organisations operate and the demands of the people around them. Among such elements, the ever-developing digital world is bound to offer novel avenues and tools to manage brands within and beyond the world of sport, allowing or even forcing brands to re-evaluate their offerings and potential audiences and target markets. At the same time, with the boundaries of sport and entertainment increasingly fading, a redefinition of sport and its brands might be already overdue, calling for a re-evaluation of strategic brand management in and through sport. Similarly, with questions on integrity and ethics being brought on the forefront, increasing pressure is expected to be placed on how brands respond, while their responsibility and actions on wider issues of the environment, the community or social activism can be also envisaged to influence brand management practice. As the Covid-19 pandemic has demonstrated, sport brands might also have a key role to play in the promotion of physical and mental wellbeing, potentially reshaping the ways in which future brand management can occur. True to the discipline's roots, the examination of these elements – alongside new unpredictable elements that will emerge – in strategic brand management in and through sport cannot but add to uncovering new and exciting aspects of sport marketing's theory and practice.

Disclosure statement

No potential conflict of interest was reported by the author(s).

ORCID

Argyro Elisavet Manoli http://orcid.org/0000-0001-7484-4124

References

Aaker, D. A. (1989). Managing assets and skills: The key to a sustainable competitive advantage. *California Management Review*, *31*(2), 91–106. https://doi.org/10.2307/41166561

Aaker, D. A. (1991). *Managing Brand Equity*. New York, NY: The Free Press.

Aaker, J. L. (1997). Dimensions of brand personality. *Journal of Marketing Research*, *34*(3), 347. https://doi.org/10.1177/002224379703400304

Bauer, H. H., Sauer, N. E., & Schmitt, P. (2005). Customer-based brand equity in the team sport industry. *European Journal of Marketing*, *39*(5/6), 496–513. https://doi.org/10.1108/03090560510590683

Doyle, J. P., Kunkel, T., Kelly, S. J., Filo, K., & Cuskelly, G. (2021). Seeing the same things differently: Exploring the unique brand associations linked to women's professional sport teams. *Journal of Strategic Marketing*, 1–15. https://doi.org/10.1080/0965254X.2021.1922489

Ehrenberg, A., Barnard, N., & Scriven, J. (1997). Differentiation or salience. *Journal of Advertising Research*, *37*(6), 7–15.

Fawbert, J. (2017). West Ham United in the Olympic Stadium: A Gramscian analysis of the rocky road to Stratford. In P. Cohen & P. Watt (Eds.), *London 2012 and the Post-Olympics City* (pp. 259–286). Palgrave Macmillan.

Fulmer, R. M. (1965). Product management: Panacea or Pandora's Box? *California Management Review*, *7*(4), 63–74. https://doi.org/10.2307/41165648

Gladden, J. M., & Funk, D. C. (2001). Understanding brand loyalty in professional sport: Examining the link between brand associations and brand loyalty. *International Journal of Sports Marketing and Sponsorship*, *3*(1), 54–81. https://doi.org/10.1108/IJSMS-03-01-2001-B006

Harris, F., & de Chernatony, L. (2001). Corporate branding and corporate brand performance. *European Journal of Marketing*, *35*(3/4), 441–456. https://doi.org/10.1108/03090560110382101

Henseler, J., Wilson, B., & Westberg, K. (2011). Managers' perceptions of the impact of sport sponsorship on brand equity: Which aspects of the sponsorship matter most? *Sport Marketing Quarterly*, *20*(1), 7–21.

Ireland, R., Muc, M., Bunn, C., & Boyland, E. (2021). Marketing of unhealthy brands during the 2018 Fédération Internationale de Football Association (FIFA) World Cup UK broadcasts – a frequency analysis. *Journal of Strategic Marketing*, 1–16. https://doi.org/10.1080/0965254X.2021.1967427

Keller, K. L. (1993). Conceptualizing, measuring, and managing customer-based brand equity. *Journal of Marketing*, *57*(1), 1–22. https://doi.org/10.1177/002224299305700101

Keller, K. L. (2003). Brand synthesis: The multidimensionality of brand knowledge. *The Journal of Consumer Research*, *29*(4), 595–600. https://doi.org/10.1086/346254

Keller, K. L. (2016). Unlocking the power of integrated marketing communications: How integrated is your IMC program? *Journal of Advertising*, *45*(3), 286–301. https://doi.org/10.1080/00913367.2016.1204967

Kenyon, J. A., Manoli, A. E., & Bodet, G. (2018). Brand consistency and coherency at the London 2012 Olympic Games. *Journal of Strategic Marketing*, *26*(1), 6–18. https://doi.org/10.1080/0965254X.2017.1293139

Kim, S., & Manoli, A. E. (2020). Building team brand equity through perceived CSR: The mediating role of dual identification. *Journal of Strategic Marketing*, 1–15. https://doi.org/10.1080/0965254X.2020.1795912

Lear, R. W. (1963). No easy road to market orientation. *Harvard Business Review*, *41*(5), 53–60.

Luxton, S., Reid, M., & Mavondo, F. (2017). IMC capability: Antecedents and implications for brand performance. *European Journal of Marketing*, *51*(3), 421–444. https://doi.org/10.1108/EJM-08-2015-0583

Manoli, A. E. (2018). Sport marketing's past, present and future; an introduction to the special issue on contemporary issues in sports marketing. *Journal of Strategic Marketing*, *26*(1), 1–5. https://doi.org/10.1080/0965254X.2018.1389492

Manoli, A. E. (2020). Brand capabilities in English premier league clubs. *European Sport Management Quarterly*, *20*(1), 30–46. https://doi.org/10.1080/16184742.2019.1693607

Manoli, A. E., & Hodgkinson, I. R. (2017). Marketing outsourcing in the English Premier League: the rights holder/agency interface. *European Sport Management Quarterly*, *17*(4), 436–456. https://doi.org/10.1080/16184742.2017.1314530

Manoli, A. E., & Hodgkinson, I. R. (2020). The implementation of integrated marketing communication (IMC): Evidence from professional football clubs in England. *Journal of Strategic Marketing*, *28*(6), 542–563. https://doi.org/10.1080/0965254X.2019.1593225

Manoli, A. E., & Kenyon, J. A. (2018). Football and marketing. In S. Chadwick, D. Parnell, P. Widdop, & C. Anagnostopoulos (Eds.), *Routledge handbook of football business and management* (pp. 88–100). Routledge.

McCarthy, J., Rowley, J., Jane Ashworth, C., & Pioch, E. (2014). Managing brand presence through social media: The case of UK football clubs. *Internet Research*, *24*(2), 181–204. https://doi.org/10.1108/IntR-08-2012-0154

Pongsakornrungsilp, S., & Schroeder, J. E. (2011). Understanding value co-creation in a co-consuming brand community. *Marketing Theory*, *11*(3), 303–324. https://doi.org/10.1177/1470593111408178

Richelieu, A. (2016). Sport teams' brands going international: The 'Integrated Marketing Strategy on the Internationalisation in Sport' (IMSIS). *Journal of Brand Strategy*, *5*(2), 218–231.

Richelieu, A., & Webb, A. (2021). Strategic sport marketing in the society of the spectacle. *Journal of Strategic Marketing*, 1–18. https://doi.org/10.1080/0965254X.2021.1965188

Schade, M., Piehler, R., & Burmann, C. (2014). Sport club brand personality scale (SCBPS): A new brand personality scale for sport clubs. *Journal of Brand Management*, *21*(7–8), 650–663. https://doi.org/10.1057/bm.2014.36

Schultz, D. E., Patti, C. H., & Kitchen, P. J. (2013). *The evolution of integrated marketing communications: The customer-driven marketplace*. Routledge.

Tezinde, T., Smith, B., & Murphy, J. (2002). Getting permission: Exploring factors affecting permission marketing. *Journal of Interactive Marketing*, *16*(4), 28–36. https://doi.org/10.1002/dir.10041

Tsordia, C., Apostolopoulou, A., & Papadimitriou, D. (2021). Does team identification of satellite fans influence brand-related sponsorships outcomes? What we learned from Manchester United supporters in Malaysia. *Journal of Strategic Marketing*, 1–19. https://doi.org/10.1080/0965254X.2021.2004208

Webb, A., & Orr, K. (2021). Strategic marketing through sport for development: Managing multi-stakeholder partnerships. *Journal of Strategic Marketing*, 1–17. https://doi.org/10.1080/0965254X.2021.1976251

Zhang, J., Jiang, Y., Shabbir, R., & Du, M. (2015). Building industrial brand equity by leveraging firm capabilities and co-creating value with customers. *Industrial Marketing Management*, *51*, 47–58. https://doi.org/10.1016/j.indmarman.2015.05.016

Seeing the same things differently: exploring the unique brand associations linked to women's professional sport teams

Jason Patrick Doyle, Thilo Kunkel, Sarah Jane Kelly, Kevin Filo and Graham Cuskelly

ABSTRACT

Sport brand management has become an increasingly strategic process, yet most scholarly attention has been focused exclusively on men's sport. This study contributes to knowledge surrounding women's sport brands and the strategic marketing of sport organizations' brand portfolios. We drew upon sport brand architecture and brand association knowledge to examine how consumers evaluate and perceive women's professional sport team brands. Data collected via free-thought listing and semi-structured interviews ($N = 31$) revealed that while established linked brands (e.g. the pre-existing men's team) help shape consumer perceptions toward women's professional sport brands, unique associations driven by social and economic factors are also linked to these brands. Findings contribute to the strategic sport brand management literature and can be used by sport organizations and their stakeholders to guide the creation and development of women's sport brand equity.

Introduction

Strategic brand management remains critical for sport marketers, who operate within a lucrative and highly competitive industry (Manoli, 2018, 2020). Sport organizations strive to develop consumer bases comprised of individuals who demonstrate support for the organization as spectators and fans. By understanding consumer perceptions of their brands, sport marketers may obtain a competitive advantage by better positioning their brands to align with the needs of consumers and their stakeholders (Daniels et al., 2019; Kenyon et al., 2018). To strategically grow, many sport organizations are increasingly investing in women's sport. In some instances, the creation and success of women's leagues and teams has occurred independently from the pre-existing men's offerings (e.g. The National Women's Soccer League [NWSL] has no backing from the men's Major Soccer League [MLS]). Elsewhere, examples from Australia and Europe document strategies where women's sport leagues and teams are introduced as extensions of the men's offerings. In either scenario, men's sport still dominates both the media and academic research (Delia, 2020; Fink, 2015), yet attendance statistics show that consumers have a strong demand for women's sport. For example, nearly 61,000 spectators attended Atletico Madrid's clash with FC Barcelona in 2019, setting a world record for domestic attendance at a women's football match. Elsewhere, the Australian Football League Women's (AFLW) competition attracted over 53,000 spectators to the 2019 final.

In many respects, Australia is leading the way by providing professional opportunities for women to play Australian Rules Football (AFLW), Rugby League (National Rugby League Women's; NRLW), Rugby Union (Super W), Soccer (W-League), Cricket (Women's Big Bash League; WBBL), and Netball (Super Netball). The dominant branding approach used in Australia is to introduce these brands as extensions of the existing men's leagues with the AFLW, NRLW, Super W, W-League and WBBL each being added to the pre-existing branded house (Kunkel & Biscaia, 2020). This is also true at the team level, where 38 of the 40 teams across the five leagues compete under the same brand identity as the men's team, consistent with how many European sport organizations position their women's teams. Whilst brand management within men's sport is relatively well understood, opportunities exist to better understand how women's sport brands are perceived by consumers (Lobpries et al., 2018). Consequently, scholars have called for further work examining women's sport (Morgan, 2019; Mumcu et al., 2016) and consumer perceptions of women's sport specifically (Delia, 2020; Sveinson & Hoeber, 2016).

Scholars highlight that strategic sport brand management should adopt a consumer-focused approach (Mumcu & Lough, 2017; Schade et al., 2014). Through the current research we facilitate an improved understanding of strategic brand management within women's sport by focusing on consumer perceptions of these brands. To achieve this aim, we conducted 31 semi-structured interviews with Australian sport consumers. We specifically explored if similarities existed within their preferences for women's and men's sport teams, and more importantly, aimed to uncover the unique brand associations these consumers link to Australian-based women's sport teams.

Literature review

Managing sport brands

Strategic brand management has become critical given the increasingly competitive nature of the sport industry, as brand creation and marketing processes both influence how consumers perceive brands (Manoli, 2020). In turn, sport organizations have adopted an increasingly strategic approach to managing their brands (Daniels et al., 2019; Kenyon et al., 2018). Research surrounding new sport teams demonstrates how consumers may attach to such entities with no pre-existing history or past success through established city or sport identifications (Fujak et al., 2020; Lock et al., 2011), or via the novelty of being a fan from the beginning (Doyle et al., 2017). Whilst this literature has provided valuable contributions to knowledge, research of this type has thus far been focused exclusively on men's sport. Given men's and women's sport can produce distinct on-field products and fan bases, and women's sport typically does not attract the magnitude of corporate support or media coverage as men's sport (e.g. Delia, 2020; Farrell, et al., 2011; Geurin,

2017), opportunities remain to determine how women's sport brands may be best managed (e.g. Sveinson & Hoeber, 2016).

Researchers have begun to explore how leagues utilize different brand development strategies to build connections with consumers (Kunkel et al., 2014). Drawing upon Ansoff's (1957) research, scholars have shown how leagues utilize market penetration (e.g. increasing sales to existing consumers), market development (e.g. extending the product to new markets), product development (e.g. modifying the core product's characteristics to appeal to existing or new consumers), or diversification (e.g. modifying the product to target a new market) strategies to manage their brands (Kunkel et al., 2014). These brand management strategies target both existing and new consumers, aligning with scholarly suggestions that sport organizations need to adopt strategic brand management practices to safeguard their brands and capitalize on new opportunities (Ströbel & Germelmann, 2020). One way that some sport leagues have chosen to strengthen their existing brands and target new opportunities has been to expand their portfolios to include women's brands. Likewise, many sponsors perceive women's sport as an authentic platform to align with and support important societal issues like gender equality as well as to create new revenue models (Morgan, 2019; Staurowsky, 2019).

Women's sport brands

Opportunities to access sport have long been biased toward men, from both a participatory and spectator perspective. For example, many professional sport leagues provide pathways for male athletes only. Whilst this imbalance is being addressed via the introduction of new women's professional leagues and teams, there are still significant questions surrounding how these entities may be best managed (Delia, 2020). Scholars posit that the motives to consume women's sport may be different to male sport contexts. Research has highlighted the influence of socialization agents, links with social causes, and perceptions of affordability represent significant factors underpinning the consumption of women's sport (Fink et al., 2002; Funk et al., 2002). Additionally, Mumcu et al. (2016) found perceptions pertaining to the ability to provide exciting and affordable entertainment were significant predictors of consumption intentions for women's sport. Delia (2020) argued that historical, economic and social conditions governing women's sport may impact how consumers identify with individual teams. Congruent with this line of thinking, the contextual factors surrounding women's sport teams may also impact how consumers perceive them, yet empirical research of this kind is limited.

Whilst brand-related research on women's sport has commenced, much of this has focused on the individual athlete (Mills, 2019). Scholars note that female athletes face substantial challenges related to accessing appropriate media coverage (Geurin, 2017) alongside unequal pay and a lack of sponsorship income (Lobpries et al., 2018; Taylor et al., 2020). Similar challenges persist at the team level, yet research on women's sport teams remains limited (Morgan, 2019). This paucity coupled with calls from scholars to better understand how consumers construct perceptions toward women's sport (Delia, 2020; Farrell et al., 2011) framed our investigation. Thus, we add to the literature by offering empirical insights into how consumers perceive and evaluate women's sport team brands. Brand architecture, discussed next, provided the theoretical lens and facilitated consideration of how consumer perceptions may be impacted by the pre-existing and related brands that surround women's sport team brands.

Brand architecture

Brand architecture provides a basis to understand the interrelationships between sport brands linked within a given portfolio (Kunkel et al., 2013). Whereas the majority of sport brand researchers have investigated sport brands at an isolated level (e.g. league, team or athlete), such brands impact one another and are inherently interlinked. These relationships are characterized by hierarchical exchanges between master-brands and sub-brands (Kunkel & Biscaia, 2020). In the sport context, leagues typically reflect the master-brand, providing the structure within which numerous sub-brands (e.g. teams and athletes) operate. Theoretically, brand architecture postulates the perceptions that consumers hold toward any given sport brand may be influenced by the other brands within the sport brand ecosystem (Daniels et al., 2019; Kunkel & Biscaia, 2020). Such brands may include other sport teams, sponsoring brands, or charitable partner brands affiliated with the team.

Anderson's (1990) research on associative networking helps to explain how consumers process information through linking nodes of information with one another. Hence, associative learning results from an updating of information based upon exposure to brand information over time, materializing in initially unconnected pieces of information being linked and strengthened to form a cognitive representation of the brand (Anderson, 1990). Research has evidenced how the presence of star players can be beneficial to helping consumers learn about the teams and leagues they play in (Shapiro et al., 2017). Similarly, sponsorship activities may influence the creation of unique associations for the respective sport brand, sponsor brand, and the sponsorship relationship (Cornwell et al., 2005). These examples illustrate how related brands may impact how a consumer perceives a given brand through associative networking links (Anderson, 1990). Researchers have demonstrated vertical co-dependencies exist between league and team brands (Kunkel et al., 2013) and between league, team and individual athlete brands (Daniels et al., 2019). However, research of this kind has yet to explore how consumers form perceptions toward women's sport brands, nor considered how other related brands may impact consumer perceptions of women's sport teams.

Brand associations

Brand associations represent any thought in the consumer's mind linked to a given brand and reflect salient attributes and benefits (Keller, 1993). For sport organizations, understanding consumer brand perceptions is an important means to improve the positioning of the brand (Kenyon et al., 2018; Manoli, 2020). Scholars have sought to uncover the range of associations consumers attach to sport teams through research spanning multiple sports and contexts (e.g. Bauer et al., 2008; Gladden & Funk, 2002; Ross et al., 2006), showing they are key predictors of consumers' attitudes, behaviors and team identification (Doyle et al., 2013; Kunkel et al., 2016; Wear & Heere, 2020). Yet, to date, this knowledge has been generated solely from investigations of men's sport. Table 1 summarizes the associations previously uncovered in men's sport research.

Table 1. Brand associations identified in men's professional sport research.

Gladden & Funk (2001)	Ross et al. (2006)	Bauer et al. (2008)	Kunkel et al. (2016)
ATTRIBUTES			
Success	Team Success	Success	Success
Star Player	-	Star Player(s)	Star Player
Head Coach	Non-Player Personnel	Head Coach	Head Coach
Management	Organizational Attributes	Management	Management
Logo	Brand Mark	Logo and Club Colors	Logo
Stadium	Stadium Community	Stadium	Stadium
Product Delivery	Team Play Characteristics	Team Performance	Product Delivery
Tradition	Team History	Club History and Tradition	-
-	-	Team Members	-
-	-	Club Culture and Values	-
-	-	Fans	-
-	-	Sponsor or Owner	-
-	-	Regional Provenance	-
BENEFITS			
Pride in Place	-	Pride in Place	Pride in Place
Escape	-	Escape	Escape
Fan Identification	Rivalry	Fan Identification	Fan Identification
Nostalgia	-	Nostalgia	-
Peer Group Acceptance	-	Peer Group Acceptance	Peer Group Acceptance
-	Social Interactions	Socialization/Companionship	-
-	Commitment	-	-
-	Concessions	-	-
-	-	Emotions	-
-	-	Entertainment	-

Examining women's sport is important as previous work demonstrates brand associations fluctuate based on consumer experiences and marketing efforts (Kunkel et al., 2016). As certain women's professional sport teams exist within pre-established brand architecture portfolios, it is likely that consumer perceptions will be influenced by related team brands (Kunkel & Biscaia, 2020). However, the relative lack of exposure and awareness of women's professional sport teams (Farrell et al., 2011) alongside numerous social, historical, and economic differences between men's and women's sport (Delia, 2020), means that consumers may also possess brand associations unique to women's sport. This is especially likely as many women's sport teams are in early stages of the product lifecycle (e.g. semi professional), and researchers have suggested the contextual factors surrounding women's sport impact how consumers engage with, and develop connections toward, such teams (Fink et al., 2002; Funk et al., 2002; Mumcu & Lough, 2017). Thus, the following research question was the focus of our investigation:

What are the unique brand associations consumers hold toward women's sport teams?

Methodology

Research context

We focused our investigation on consumers of women's professional sport in Australia. This research setting was selected because the predominant strategy employed to introduce women's sport teams in Australia has been via brand extensions. For example, the Sydney Roosters play in both the men's NRL and the women's NRLW leagues. When the Sydney Roosters women's team was introduced in 2018, the same branding as the men's team (established in 1908) was leveraged and adopted across the women's team brand. As such, this context provided an opportune setting to conduct our research.

Sample and data collection

Thirty-one semi-structured interviews were conducted. We utilized a purposive sampling method whereby recruitment occurred via social media posts placed by the lead researcher across their personal and departmental accounts. These posts invited individuals who self-identified as fans of women's sport to contact the research team. Interviews were held in-person and each participant received a $25 AUD supermarket voucher as a thank you for their time. After the thirty-first interview, no new themes or concepts were emerging, suggesting theoretical saturation had been reached. Seventeen respondents identified as female (54.8%), and fourteen respondents identified as male (45.2%). The mean age was 35.25 years, ranging from 22 to 71 years. Interviews ranged from 20 to 57 minutes, averaging 36 minutes. In total, 18 hours and 39 minutes of audio data were transcribed into text.

Measurement

The interviews commenced with each respondent completing a short survey. Respondents were asked to provide their demographic information and to indicate their favorite women's sport team, from any sport and country, using an open text box. For comparative purposes, we also asked respondents to indicate their favorite men's team, from any sport and country. Respondents then indicated their level of fandom toward both on a scale of 1 – Casual Observer to 7 – Hardcore Fanatic (Na et al., 2019). Next, drawing from brand association research (Kunkel et al., 2014), each respondent was asked to think about their favorite women's sport team and to complete a free-thought listing exercise. This consisted of listing the most salient associations that emerged when thinking of the team. To gain richer insight into the associations listed, the respondents were asked to explain why they linked each association with the team during the interview phase of the research. To elicit rich data, probing questions including asking respondents to provide examples of how their listed associations applied to their stated teams were utilized.

Results

As illustrated in Table 2, the sample's team preferences were dynamic and in many cases differed between sports. Paired sample t-tests revealed respondents reported generally stronger connections ($t(30) = 2.425$, $p = .022$) with their favorite men's team ($M = 5.26$, $SD = 1.154$) as opposed to their favorite women's team ($M = 4.45$, $SD = 1.609$). Specifically, 18 respondents (58%) reported a stronger level of fandom with their nominated men's team, 8 respondents (25.9%) had a stronger connection with their favorite women's team, and five respondents (16.1%) reported the same level of fandom for both. Interestingly,

Table 2. Respondent demographics and favourite team selections.

Pseudonym	Age	Gender	Favourite Women's Team (Year Established)	Level of Fandom	Favourite Men's Team (Year Established)	Level of Fandom
Jacinta	24	Female	Brisbane Heat (2015)	5	Brisbane Broncos (1988)	4
Zoe	22	Female	Sydney Sixers (2015)	2	Canberra Raiders (1981)	5
Jill	27	Female	Brisbane Roar (2008)	4	Gold Coast Titans (2007)	2
Shelly	23	Female	Gold Coast Suns (2017)	3	Brisbane Broncos (1988)	3
Fleur	30	Female	Brisbane Roar (2008)	7	Brisbane Roar (1957)	4
Vanessa	54	Female	Brisbane Roar (2008)	6	Melbourne Storm (1997)	6
Crystal	32	Female	Matildas (1975)	7	Socceroos (1922)	5
Chloe	25	Female	Brisbane Lions (2016)	3	Brisbane Bullets (1979)	5
Rachel	71	Female	Brisbane Roar (2008)	6	Brisbane Broncos (1988)	6
Hannah	34	Female	Brisbane Lions (2016)	4	Brisbane Lions (1996)	6
Jolene	31	Female	Queensland Reds (2018)	5	Melbourne Rebels (2010)	6
Kimberly	27	Female	Jillaroos (1995)	4	South Sydney Rabbitohs (1908)	5
Natalie	59	Female	Brisbane Roar (2008)	6	Parramatta Eels (1946)	6
Melissa	26	Female	Brisbane Roar (2008)	6	Brisbane Roar (1957)	5
Sally	22	Female	Queensland Reds (2018)	5	Brisbane Lions (1996)	4
Rose	37	Female	Brisbane Roar (2008)	6	Brisbane Broncos (1988)	5
Marilyn	52	Female	Brisbane Roar (2008)	7	Heart of Midlothian (1874)	6
Magnus	29	Male	Gold Coast Suns (2017)	3	Gold Coast Titans (2007)	6
Teddy	35	Male	Matildas (1975)	4	Manchester United (1878)	6
Kane	30	Male	Brisbane Heat (2015)	5	Brisbane Broncos (1988)	7
Stefan	27	Male	Brisbane Broncos (2018)	5	Brisbane Broncos (1988)	5
Jackson	34	Male	Queensland Reds (2018)	1	Queensland Reds (1882)	4
Barney	26	Male	Brisbane Roar (2008)	2	Brisbane Roar (1957)	6
Jeff	26	Male	Matildas (1975)	1	Liverpool FC (1892)	6
Campbell	27	Male	Brisbane Heat (2015)	5	Gold Coast Titans (2007)	7
Alex	39	Male	Brisbane Lions (2016)	4	Brisbane Lions (1996)	5
Greg	58	Male	QLD Firebirds (1997)	5	Scotland Rugby Union Team (1871)	7
Callum	32	Male	Australian Cricket Team (1934)	5	Brisbane Broncos (1988)	6
Patrick	55	Male	Brisbane Heat (2015)	4	Brisbane Lions (1996)	5
Dante	45	Male	Brisbane Roar (2008)	4	West Bromwich Albion (1878)	4
Murphy	34	Male	Brisbane Lions (2016)	4	Collingwood Magpies (1892)	6

approximately one-in-three respondents (29%) indicated following a favorite women's team that was in the same brand portfolio as the men's team. Of these nine respondents, four (44.4%) indicated a greater bond with the women's team and five (55.5%) respondents indicated a stronger connection with the men's team.

To address the research question, we followed Creswell's (2009) suggestions to interpret the data. First, we generated a list of associations for each respondent based on the associations they listed and their subsequent interview transcript. For example, if a respondent listed the name of a player (e.g. Ellyse Perry) as a team association, this was designated as 'Star Player'. We initially adopted a deductive approach cross-referencing the associations uncovered in prior literature. In this initial phase of coding, a number of the associations identified within men's professional sport research (e.g. Star Player and Success) emerged. As these are well established associations and validation of previous work was not our focus, we reviewed the data to uncover previously unidentified themes in the second step. Evidence of five new brand associations not previously identified in men's professional sport research emerged. Three of these associations represented positive associations, whereas the other two represented negative associations. Each of these is now discussed and accompanied by illustrative quotes.

The first new association identified was titled *Diversity and Inclusion*. This reflected an acknowledgement that the team was welcoming to all and was evident amongst both players and fans. Chloe spoke positively about the team's approach to building a diverse roster commenting 'They take a lot of girls from different, assorted backgrounds.' Dante held similar thoughts related to how the team fostered an inclusive environment within the supporter base, and contrasted this with perceptions of the men's team stating:

> They're very inclusive ... Everyone can feel like they're part of it. I think the men's league might be quite "blokey", [but here] there's a real range of people. You get obviously a large amount of people from the LGBTQ community, you get older people, younger people, kids who play football - a mix of people.

The second association, *Role Models*, captured perceptions that the team's players set a good example for others. Respondents spoke about this with respect to the players' professional and private lives. Alex stated that 'Girls can now look up to the women playing football and say, "I can be that and I can do that."' Dante shared a similar perspective:

> Grassroots [football] is really growing, especially for girls. They have people to idolize and who they want to be like ... It gives girls who want to play football someone to look up to, and they're role models outside of football with their fulltime jobs.

Callum further commented on this aspect stating:

> The women just don't seem to play up like the men do ... I don't think I've ever seen a women's player in any sport for that matter on the back page of [newspaper] because they've been in a drunken fight at the pub.

The third association, *Funding Limitations*, reflected perceptions that the team was operating despite significant financial challenges. This perception was related to team budgets and player salaries. Commenting on team budgets Marilyn said: 'The money that they spend on the women compared to the men is absolutely ridiculous, and some of the terms and conditions that the women have to put up with compared to what the men get are a disgrace.' Referencing player salaries, Hannah noted: 'It's hard to be a professional sportswoman in Australia – there are huge disparities between men's and women's sport. I don't think there's many women who play professional sport as their sole occupation and earn enough money to be comfortable.' Vanessa also spoke about this disparity, noting: 'These women dedicate their lives for not much money. They're not even on minimum wage!'

The fourth association, *Lack of Coverage*, captured difficulties in following the team due to limited media coverage. This was true with respect to watching team games and accessing team information more generally. Campbell noted that the lack of coverage usually saw the women's games being available only as replays, but 'watching a live game compared to watching a replay game is completely different.' Additionally, Callum commented 'The NRLW [is] not televised very much' and Marilyn stated media coverage surrounding their favorite women's team was 'decades behind the men's.' Beyond the team's games, Shelly wanted more internet and social media news, as well as being able to purchase women's team merchandise. Shelly said:

> You constantly see advertising on Facebook and Google for men's football ... But you don't really see the same thing for the women ... Even when you go online and you go to buy something from [the team's website], they don't really emphasize the women's side of it.

The fifth association, *New Opportunities*, identified how the team opened up broader opportunities for women and girls in sport. These opportunities were identified at both grassroots and elite levels. Jacinta saw the opportunities the professional teams afforded at the grassroots level and how this differed from her own experience as a junior participant saying:

> I love that women are getting more opportunity, which is translating down to a grassroots level. For me, as a child, there wasn't as much opportunity. You went from playing [junior] boy's cricket to playing [senior] women's - there wasn't a good transition in between.

Chloe also commented on how opportunities at the professional level impacted the pathway for juniors, saying: 'At my club, every age group for girls now has a team. The under 11s to 17s – it's really growing. We have a good grassroots program where they can start that pathway up to the women's [professional team].' Finally, Callum commented that the new opportunities and pathways acted as a means for young women to pursue sport for health and career-related purposes, noting:

> In a country that has such an obesity problem, I am all for anything that's going to promote physical activity to a much wider audience. Especially for young girls. To see that there's a path for them if they wanted to remain physically active, or that they can pursue professional sport as a career.

Discussion

This study drew upon brand architecture and brand association literature to explore how consumers perceive women's sport team brands. Our findings support the conceptual propositions of sport brand architecture (Kunkel & Biscaia, 2020) and extend knowledge by demonstrating how multi-gendered sport brands are perceived by consumers based on previous brand experiences and knowledge (e.g. Daniels et al., 2019). Approximately one-third of our sample (29%) indicated their favorite men's and women's sport team was from the same brand portfolio, with the majority of the sample (71%) reporting dissimilar preferences, which in many cases crossed over different sports. This finding supports the notion that sport consumers buy from a repertoire of brands (Fujak et al., 2018) and helps to identify key consumer-based aspects upon which women's sport brands can be strategically managed (Delia, 2020; Taylor et al., 2020). Overall, these findings suggest that consumer perceptions towards women's sport brands may be somewhat informed by their pre-existing thoughts about the established men's offering, but that these brands are distinct entities which require an individualized and strategic approach towards marketing.

Our findings revealed that consumers attach additional and unique associations to women's professional sport team brands, which have not been identified previously in men's sport research (e.g. Bauer et al., 2008; Gladden & Funk, 2002; Ross et al., 2006). Interestingly, two of the five associations uncovered – *Funding Limitations* and *Lack of Coverage*, reflect negative perceptions associated with the general support provided to women's sport teams, with previous research on men's sport uncovering associations which are solely positive. These associations demonstrate how historical, economic and societal conditions impact consumer perceptions of women's brands (Delia, 2020; Farrell et al., 2011). The other three associations (*Diversity and Inclusion, Role Models*, and *New Opportunities*) were positive in nature and provide insight into how women's sport brands can be promoted effectively. Previous research outlines how individuals may be motivated to consume women's sport due to the philanthropic and social contributions made by women's teams (Fink et al., 2002; Funk et al., 2002; Mumcu & Lough, 2017), alongside the influence of corporate social responsibility in sport in fostering team identification and increasing brand equity (Kim & Manoli, 2020).

By identifying *Diversity and Inclusion, Role Models*, and *New Opportunities* as brand associations consumers attach to women's sport brands our findings support and advance previous assertions (Fink et al., 2002; Funk et al., 2002; Kim & Manoli, 2020). Similarly, the identification of the *Funding Limitations* and *Lack of Coverage* brand associations suggest long-standing inequities within women's sport influence how consumers perceive women's sport brands at the team level (Farrell et al., 2011; Geurin, 2017; Taylor et al., 2020). In terms of theoretical contributions, these new brand associations contribute a more detailed understanding of the particular opportunities and challenges women's sport organizations face in a highly competitive market. Overall, these new associations can be leveraged (positive associations) or mitigated (negative associations) by sport marketers in creating distinct and attractive brands to positively influence consumer attitudes and behaviors (Doyle et al., 2013; Kunkel et al., 2016; Wear & Heere, 2020).

Implications

Our findings highlight how women's sport brands face additional branding challenges not evidenced within men's sport research. We also uncover areas where women's sport brands may be able to positively differentiate from existing men's offerings. Collectively, this work can be used to guide brand development strategies to help organizations gain a competitive advantage for individual brands and for their broader brand portfolios (Kenyon et al., 2018). These findings can inform marketing practices regarding how women's sport brands can develop and promote points of differentiation with men's offerings. In particular, promoting players as *Role Models* and their teams as champions of *Diversity and Inclusion* paving the way to create *New Opportunities* are aspects that brand managers should emphasize when seeking to enhance the economic value of women's sport team brands (e.g. Funk et al., 2002, 2003). This marketing could be developed to engage further with both new and existing customers (Ansoff, 1957; Kunkel et al., 2014) and to enhance the appeal of the organization to sponsors and government stakeholders.

Women's sport teams should emphasize the elements of *Diversity and Inclusion*, *Role Models*, and *New Opportunities* prominently within their marketing and communication strategies. Our findings suggest that these aspects represent unique and favorable associations through which a competitive advantage may be obtained. Given consumers' appreciation of sport organizations who are aligned with charitable causes (Fink et al., 2002), showcasing the team's on-field accomplishments and the social value of the team may increase their corporate and commercial appeal as per research in the league context (Mumcu & Lough, 2017). For example, the U.S Women's National Soccer Team are well known for their excellent on-field results and their commitment to diversity and inclusion issues and causes via lobbying for equal pay and conditions. Highlighting aspects related to the team's *Role Models* may increase a sport organization's appeal to a potential sponsor wishing to associate with a wholesome image, while promoting the team's ability to provide *New Opportunities* for women and girls in sport may appeal to government and funding bodies. Government campaigns like 'This Girl Can' in the UK (Sport England, 2015) and 'Girls Make Your Move' in Australia (Australian Government, 2018) have encouraged more women and girls to become involved in sport as a means to improve public health, social cohesion, and contribute to the economy. Our findings may help sport organizations access additional resources through such initiatives, combating the additional challenges associated with *Funding Limitations* and the *Lack of Coverage* impacting the marketing of women's sport brands (e.g. Fink, 2015).

These findings may also assist sponsors of women's sport in leveraging their sponsorships. Women's sport brands provide a genuine opportunity for sponsors to authentically engage with both economic and cause-related marketing objectives in mind (e.g. Cornwell, 2019). As consumers attach additional positive attributes to women's sport brands (e.g. *Diversity and Inclusion, Role Models, New Opportunities*), affiliation with women's sport brands may be perceived positively and differentiate sponsors from those sponsoring men's teams (e.g. Kim & Manoli, 2020) helping to influence consumer attitudes and behaviors toward these sponsoring brands. The clear demand for women's sport, as demonstrated by ever-increasing viewership and global popularity further demonstrates how investment in women's sport can help organizations diversify their sponsorship portfolios and produce a positive return on their investment (Delia, 2020; Morgan, 2019). Such investment in women's sport may also help authentically demonstrate a sponsor's commitment to diversity and inclusion initiatives (Cornwell, 2019) and in showing appreciation for the sponsor's customers and the team's fanbase.

Limitations and future research

This study offers direction for future research which can address some of the limitations of our work. First, we conducted exploratory research assessing the perceptions of a sample of Australian-based consumers. As consumer-based brand associations can be context-specific, researchers should examine different settings including where men's and women's professional teams are branded similarly and as distinct entities. Additional research exploring the reasons why consumers do, and do not, follow men's and women's teams from within the same portfolio of brands is also needed to help explain the influence of these brands on one another.

Second, studies adopting quantitative methods are also encouraged to assess and build on our findings. This study leveraged an exploratory method and gathered data from a relatively small sample of consumers. Thus, larger quantitative work is needed to operationalize and test the strength to which consumers perceive each newly identified brand association, as well as to determine how associations previously uncovered in men's sport (see Table 1) are perceived in the women's sport context. Scale development work embracing research assessing the salience, valence, and interrelatedness amongst perceptions of brands within a portfolio comprised of both women's and men's brands is particularly encouraged.

Conclusion

This exploratory study contributes to strategic brand management knowledge both in and through sport, by examining consumer perceptions of women's sport team brands. Using a free-thought listing activity and semi-structured interviews, we demonstrate the impact of pre-existing brands on consumer perceptions, whilst also highlighting how such brands need to be marketed as distinct entities. The former contributes to theory surrounding brand architecture and brand association knowledge, whereas the latter offers direction to marketers within women's sport organizations. Sponsors can also be guided by our findings, which sets the foundation for further work in this under-examined but important area of brand management research.

Disclosure statement

No potential conflict of interest was reported by the author(s).

Funding

This work was supported by Griffith University's Griffith Business School as part of the New Researcher Grant initiative. We would also like to thank Dr. Michelle Hayes for assistance with data collection.

ORCID

Jason Patrick Doyle http://orcid.org/0000-0002-5049-9407
Thilo Kunkel http://orcid.org/0000-0002-1607-0148
Sarah Jane Kelly http://orcid.org/0000-0002-4664-5248
Kevin Filo http://orcid.org/0000-0001-6442-3166
Graham Cuskelly http://orcid.org/0000-0001-9352-1873

References

Anderson, J. R. (1990). *The adaptive character of thought*. Psychology Press.

Ansoff, H. I. (1957). Strategies for diversification. *Harvard Business Review*, *35*(5), 113–124. https://www.casrilanka.com/casl/images/stories/2017/2017_pdfs/sab_portal/course_material/strategies_for_diversification.pdf

Australian Government. (2018). *Girls make your move*. https://campaigns.health.gov.au/girlsmove/campaign-backgrounder

Bauer, H. H., Stokburger-Sauer, N. E., & Exler, S. (2008). Brand image and fan loyalty in professional team sport: A refined model and empirical assessment. *Journal of Sport Management*, *22*(2), 205–226. https://doi.org/10.1123/jsm.22.2.205

Cornwell, T. B. (2019). Less "sponsorship as advertising" and more sponsorship-linked marketing as authentic engagement. *Journal of Advertising*, *48*(1), 49–60. https://doi.org/10.1080/00913367.2019.1588809

Cornwell, T. B., Weeks, C. S., & Roy, D. P. (2005). Sponsorship-linked marketing: Opening the black box. *Journal of Advertising*, *34*(2), 21–42. https://doi.org/10.1080/00913367.2005.10639194

Creswell, J. W. (2009). Mapping the field of mixed methods research. *Journal of Mixed Methods Research*, *3*(2), 95–108. https://doi.org/10.1177/1558689808330883

Daniels, J., Kunkel, T., & Karg, A. (2019). New brands: Contextual differences and development of brand associations over time. *Journal of Sport Management*, *33*(2), 133–147. https://doi.org/10.1123/jsm.2018-0218

Delia, E. B. (2020). The psychological meaning of team among fans of women's sport. *Journal of Sport Management*, *34*(6), 579–590. https://doi.org/10.1123/jsm.2019-0404.

Doyle, J. P., Filo, K., McDonald, H., & Funk, D. C. (2013). Exploring sport brand double jeopardy: The link between team market share and attitudinal loyalty. *Sport Management Review*, *16*(3), 285–297. https://doi.org/10.1016/j.smr.2012.11.001

Doyle, J. P., Lock, D., Funk, D. C., Filo, K., & McDonald, H. (2017). 'I was there from the start': The identity-maintenance strategies used by fans to combat the threat of losing. *Sport Management Review*, *20*(2), 184–197. https://doi.org/10.1016/j.smr.2016.04.006

Farrell, A., Fink, J. S., & Fields, S. (2011). Women's sport spectatorship: An exploration of men's influence. *Journal of Sport Management*, *25*(3), 190–201. https://doi.org/10.1123/jsm.25.3.190

Fink, J. S. (2015). Female athletes, women's sport, and the sport media commercial complex: Have we really "come a long way, baby"? *Sport Management Review*, *18*(3), 331–342. https://doi.org/10.1016/j.smr.2014.05.001

Fink, J. S., Trail, G. T., & Anderson, D. F. (2002). Environmental factors associated with spectator attendance and sport consumption behavior: Gender and team differences. *Sport Marketing Quarterly*, *11*(1), 8–19.

Fujak, H., Frawley, S., Lock, D., & Adair, D. (2020). Consumer behaviour toward a new league and teams: Television audiences as a measure of market acceptance. *European Sport Management Quarterly*, 1–21. https://doi.org/10.1080/16184742.2020.1770310

Fujak, H., Frawley, S., McDonald, H., & Bush, S. (2018). Are sport consumers unique? Consumer behavior within crowded sport markets. *Journal of Sport Management*, *32*(4), 362–375. https://doi.org/10.1123/jsm.2017-0318

Funk, D. C., Mahony, D. F., & Ridinger, L. L. (2002). Characterizing consumer motivation as individual difference factors: Augmenting the sports interest inventory (SII) to explain level of spectator support. *Sport Marketing Quarterly*, *11*(1), 33–43. https://digitalcommons.odu.edu/hms_fac_pubs/34/

Funk, D. C., Ridinger, L. L., & Moorman, A. M. (2003). Understanding consumer support: Extending the Sport Interest Inventory (SII) to examine individual differences among women's professional sport consumers. *Sport Management Review*, *6*(1), 1–31. https://doi.org/10.1016/S1441-3523(03)70051-5

Geurin, A. N. (2017). Elite female athletes' perceptions of new media use relating to their careers: A qualitative analysis. *Journal of Sport Management*, *31*(4), 345–359. https://doi.org/10.1123/jsm.2016-0157

Gladden, J. M., & Funk, D. C. (2001). Understanding brand loyalty in professional sport: Examining the link between brand associations and brand loyalty. *International Journal of Sports Marketing and Sponsorship*, 3(1), 54–81.

Gladden, J. M., & Funk, D. C. (2002). Developing an understanding of brand associations in team sport: Empirical evidence from consumers of professional sport. *Journal of Sport Management*, 16(1), 54–81. https://doi.org/10.1123/jsm.16.1.54

Keller, K. L. (1993). Conceptualizing, measuring, and managing customer-based brand equity. *Journal of Marketing*, 57(1), 1–22. https://doi.org/10.1177/002224299305700101

Kenyon, J. A., Manoli, A. E., & Bodet, G. (2018). Brand consistency and coherency at the London 2012 Olympic Games. *Journal of Strategic Marketing*, 26(1), 6–18. https://doi.org/10.1080/0965254X.2017.1293139

Kim, S., & Manoli, A. E. (2020). Building team brand equity through perceived CSR: The mediating role of dual identification. *Journal of Strategic Marketing*, 1–15. https://doi.org/10.1080/0965254X.2020.1795912

Kunkel, T., & Biscaia, R. (2020). Sport brands - brand relationships and consumer behavior. *Sport Marketing Quarterly*, 29(1), 3–16. https://doi.org/10.32731/SMQ.291.032020.01

Kunkel, T., Doyle, J. P., & Funk, D. C. (2014). Exploring sport brand development strategies to strengthen consumer involvement with the product–the case of the Australian A-league. *Sport Management Review*, 17(4), 470–483. https://doi.org/10.1016/j.smr.2014.01.004

Kunkel, T., Doyle, J. P., Funk, D. C., Du, J., & McDonald, H. (2016). The development and change of brand associations and their influence on team loyalty over time. *Journal of Sport Management*, 30(2), 117–134. https://doi.org/10.1123/jsm.2015-0129

Kunkel, T., Funk, D., & Hill, B. (2013). Brand architecture, drivers of consumer involvement, and brand loyalty with professional sport leagues and teams. *Journal of Sport Management*, 27(3), 177–192. https://doi.org/10.1123/jsm.27.3.177

Lobpries, J., Bennett, G., & Brison, N. (2018). How I perform is not enough: Exploring branding barriers faced by elite female athletes. *Sport Marketing Quarterly*, 27(1), 5–17. https://doi.org/10.32731/SMQ.271.032018.01

Lock, D., Taylor, T., & Darcy, S. (2011). In the absence of achievement: The formation of new team identification. *European Sport Management Quarterly*, 11(2), 171–192. https://doi.org/10.1080/16184742.2011.559135

Manoli, A. E. (2018). Sport marketing's past, present and future; an introduction to the special issue on contemporary issues in sports marketing. *Journal of Strategic Marketing*, 26(1), 1–5. https://doi.org/10.1080/0965254X.2018.1389492

Manoli, A. E. (2020). Strategic brand management in and through sport. *Journal of Strategic Marketing*, 28(4), 285–287. https://doi.org/10.1080/0965254X.2020.1740420

Mills, I. (2019). Branding in women's sports: A literature review. *The Sport Journal*, 22(1), 1–7. https://thesportjournal.org/article/branding-in-womens-sports-a-literature-review/#more-6694

Morgan, A. (2019). An examination of women's sport sponsorship: A case study of female Australian rules football. *Journal of Marketing Management*, 35(17–18), 1644–1666. https://doi.org/10.1080/0267257X.2019.1668463

Mumcu, C., & Lough, N. L. (2017). Are fans proud of the WNBA's pride campaign? *Sport Marketing Quarterly*, 26(1), 42–54. https://digitalcommons.newhaven.edu/sportmanagement-facpubs/5/

Mumcu, C., Lough, N. L., & Barnes, J. C. (2016). Examination of women's sports fans' attitudes and consumption intentions. *Journal of Applied Sport Management*, 8(4), 25–47. https://doi.org/10.18666/JASM-2016-V8-I4-7221

Na, S., Su, Y., & Kunkel, T. (2019). Do not bet on your favourite football team: The influence of fan identity-based biases and sport context knowledge on game prediction accuracy. *European Sport Management Quarterly*, 19(3), 396–418. https://doi.org/10.1080/16184742.2018.1530689

Ross, S. D., James, J. D., & Vargas, P. (2006). Development of a scale to measure team brand associations in professional sport. *Journal of Sport Management*, 20(2), 260–279. https://doi.org/10.1123/jsm.20.2.260

Schade, M., Piehler, R., & Burmann, C. (2014). Sport club brand personality scale (SCBPS): A new brand personality scale for sport clubs. *Journal of Brand Management, 21*(7–8), 650–663. https://doi.org/10.1057/bm.2014.36

Shapiro, S. L., DeSchriver, T. D., & Rascher, D. A. (2017). The Beckham effect: Examining the longitudinal impact of a star performer on league marketing, novelty, and scarcity. *European Sport Management Quarterly, 17*(5), 610–634. https://doi.org/10.1080/16184742.2017.1329331

Sport England. (2015). *This girl can*. https://www.thisgirlcan.co.uk/

Staurowsky, E. J. (2019). The impact of Title IX and other equity laws on the business of women's sport. In *Routledge handbook of the business of women's sport* (Lough, N. & Geurin A.N., E.ds.,). Routledge International Handbooks

Ströbel, T., & Germelmann, C. C. (2020). Exploring new routes within brand research in sport management: Directions and methodological approaches. *European Sport Management Quarterly, 20*(1), 1–9. https://doi.org/10.1080/16184742.2019.1706603

Sveinson, K., & Hoeber, L. (2016). Female sport fans' experiences of marginalization and empowerment. *Journal of Sport Management, 30*(1), 8–21. https://doi.org/10.1123/jsm.2014-0221

Taylor, T., Fujak, H., Hanlon, C., & O'Connor, D. (2020). A balancing act: Women players in a new semi-professional team sport league. *European Sport Management Quarterly*, 1–21. https://doi.org/10.1080/16184742.2020.1815821

Wear, H., & Heere, B. (2020). Brand new: A longitudinal investigation of brand associations as drivers of team identity among fans of a new sport team. *Journal of Sport Management, 34*(5), 475–487. https://doi.org/10.1123/jsm.2018-0204

Building team brand equity through perceived CSR: the mediating role of dual identification

Sungkyung Kim and Argyro Elisavet Manoli

ABSTRACT
While involvement in CSR activities is common practice in today's sporting world, there is a need to go beyond the activities themselves to explore how fans' perceptions of CSR can affect customer-based brand equity and what role online community and team identification can play in this relationship, which this study aims to explore. Data collected through an online survey of South Korean Samsung Lions baseball club fans (N = 331), analysed through structural equation modelling, support the positive influence of perceived CSR on dual identification (team and online community), and the impact of team identification on brand equity. Interestingly, CSR perception is shown to be an insignificant predictor of brand equity, influenced fully by team identification. This study suggests that promoting a sport team's socially responsible image is important in terms of building both team and online community identification while developing team identification can be vital in increasing the value of the sport brand.

1. Introduction

Brand equity has emerged as a key theme underpinning the value of the brand. Corporate social responsibility (CSR) plays an important role not only in brand equity building but also in influencing consumers' supporting behavioural intentions (Hur et al., 2014; Martínez & Nishiyama, 2017; Woo & Jin, 2016). Within the context of sport, CSR can be nowadays considered a common trend in practice and a popular academic inquiry area, with extensive research on CSR in sport and its role in society (Chang et al., 2016). Sport provides an ideal environment for CSR promotion due to its social interaction and close connection with the local community (Manoli, 2015).However, empirical evidence of the formation of sport fan-based brand equity through fans' perception of CSR has yet to be explicitly studied.

Brand management literature supports that brand equity is largely predicated on customer-company identification (Bhattacharya & Sen, 2003; Manoli, 2020), while in sport, the effect of sport fans' identification towards a team on brand equity has drawn particular attention (Wang & Tang, 2018; Watkins, 2014). However, there is scant research on identification with fans' online community in understanding brand equity despite the enormous value online communities yield sport entities. It is worth acknowledging that emotional attachment to the sport fans' community was shown to be a robust predictor of team identification and positive behavioural intentions such as future attendance (Yoshida et al., 2015). Furthermore, the use of online-based communication techniques by sport organisations to communicate team and player news in real-time has enabled them to promote CSR initiatives further and quicker, allowing them to influence perception and attitude of sport fans (Morrison et al., 2018).

It is also worth noting that sport fans have multiple relationships within a community: horizontal relationships between fans and vertical relationships with the team they support. Although building the horizontal connection, fan-to-fan relationships, is sometimes more important than the vertical connection in understanding fan behaviour, there are few empirical studies to support the idea (Katz & Heere, 2015; Katz et al., 2018). Moreover, given the fact that an individual can develop multiple identities in the process of becoming a sport fan, it is crucial to examine the formation of sport team brand equity from the multiple targets of identification (Wang & Tang, 2018). Since members in the online community intrinsically connected with the team, identification with the community and the team should be distinguished. By doing so, brand managers of sport teams can design different strategies depending on the different targets of identification. Despite the fact that the firm and the intertwined link between an organisation (team), consumer(fan), and community (Walker & Kent, 2009), online community identification is still a missing piece of the puzzle in that relationship.

To fill these gaps, this study aims to investigate the links among perceived CSR, fan's team and online community identification, and brand equity, in an attempt to further our understanding of building and managing customer-based brand equity for sport organisations. The manuscript is structured as follows; first, the existing literature linking the four areas is reviewed, before the hypotheses and the conceptual framework of our study are presented. Next, the sample, data collection and measurement details are outlined. Then the results of our study are presented before its implications and limitations are considered while highlighting future research avenues.

Literature review and hypotheses development

CSR and team identification

Identification towards a sport team has its academic roots in social identity theory, indicating an individual's perception that they belong to a social group. At the same time, social identity theory is often seen as an outcome of CSR. Organisations put much effort into promoting diverse CSR initiatives to meet the expectations of society and to encourage consumers to build a level of social identity with them (Manoli, 2015, 2018). Several empirical studies have confirmed that a sport team's CSR activities will result in enhancing the fan's identification with the team (Chang et al., 2016; Morrison et al., 2018). Chang et al. (2016) explored the structural relationship among sport fans' perceived CSR of teams, team identification and pride. According to the results, although CSR was not directly related to team identification, pride played a mediating role in this relationship, thus creating a link between the two. Support for linking sport teams' CSR promotion with team identification is also found in the work of Morrison et al. (2018), who tested the relationship between perception of CSR, team identification and spectator behaviour. The results demonstrated that the mediation effect of team identification on CSR and patronage behaviour was partially significant, meaning that spectators become loyal to a team in the form of repeat purchase, media consumption, merchandise consumption and positive word-of-mouth when they perceive CSR programs through team identification. Similarly, Walker and Kent (2009) confirmed that sport fans had a sense of affiliation and favourable attitude when they were aware of their team's sustained participation in goodwill activities. Therefore, this study hypothesized that:

Hypothesis 1–1. Perception of CSR is positively associated with team identification.

CSR and online community identification

Little research exists examining how perceptions of CSR have an impact on forming and strengthening members' online sport fan community identification, despite the value of the online community as a great fan-to-fan communication platform. The online community is considered an effective way of marketing communication, shifting the focus from an off-line consumption experience to an online community-based experience (Bhattacharya & Sen, 2003). Online communities are places where beneficial long-term vertical connections and horizontal connections (Katz & Heere, 2015) can be fostered simultaneously. Recently, the horizontal connection, fan-to-fan relationships, within communities has started gaining attention in the online community context. Yoshida et al. (2015) identified that attachment towards the community is a more salient predictor of attendance than team identification. This finding is underpinned by Katz et al.'s (2018) result that fan's relationships with other fans are a stronger predictor of attendance than the relationship with the team.

Although the relationship between sport fans' perception of CSR and online community identification remains under-researched, it can be inferred from existing brand marketing studies. Recent research pointed out that online community identification is a major decisive factor of community members' attitude and behavioural intentions toward both the community and the brand (Popp & Woratschek, 2017). For instance, identification with the online community has been identified as an immediate antecedent of loyalty and cooperation, trust, and engagement, and community promotion (Kim & Kim, 2017). Thus, the higher the levels of identification with a particular online community, the more expected the members are to be emotionally attached to the community, and the more likely they are to have a positive attitude and to be more loyal to both the community and the brand. Accordingly, the following hypothesis was proposed:

Hypothesis 1–2. Perception of CSR is positively associated with online community identification.

CSR and brand equity

Sport teams' brand equity is often understood as the value that fans attach to the team they support and associate with its name, players, and symbols (Gladden & Milne, 1999). For sport branding, much of a team's value comes from fans' experiences of interacting with the team, and this experience builds brand awareness and associations that result in brand equity (Watkins, 2014). Understanding brand equity is, thus, useful for sport brand managers since it allows insight on how to influence their fans' association with the team (Gladden & Milne, 1999).

Sport teams' CSR efforts are viewed as an antecedent of fan-based brand equity in the current study since sport consumers' perception of CSR activities is most likely associated with positive attitudes and behavioural intentions (e.g. loyalty, purchase intention), which are components of brand equity (Morrison et al., 2018; Walker & Kent, 2009). Evidence of the link can be inferred from research focusing on different sectors (e.g. Fatma et al., 2015; Woo & Jin, 2016), which have confirmed the efficacy of CSR initiatives on developing brand equity among consumers. Taking this lack of relevant research in sport brands into consideration, it is worth taking a look at the online fan community members' CSR-brand equity association for the expansion and further understanding of the area. Therefore, this study hypothesised a link between CSR and brand equity:

Hypothesis 2. Perceptionof CSR is positively associated with brand equity.

Team identification and brand equity

Watkins (2014) applied the social identity-brand equity (SIBE) model, originally developed by Underwood et al. (2001), in order to study the antecedents of brand equity in the context of professional sport, revealing that salient group, community group and venue are found to be predictors of fan identification, and this fan identification has a significant impact on customer-based brand equity. Through the results, the study highlighted a consumer–brand relationship that can facilitate brand equity, which is increased by fans' connection to the team (Watkins, 2014). Wang and Tang (2018) extended Watkins (2014) research framework by proposing a dual-identification model (identification with sport team and identification with sport team brand) to examine the dual identification as an antecedent of sport team brand equity. Wang and Tang (2018) tested both sport team and sport team identification since professional baseball teams in Taiwan are run by a wider umbrella company, whose name is even used as part of the team's name. Their results indicated that both sport team identification and sport team brand identification were significant predictors of sport team brand equity. The study confirmed that identification with a team and with a brand concurrently creates sport team brand equity.

Boyle and Magnusson (2007) also adopted the SIBE model as a conceptual framework and classified a college team's fan groups into current students, alumni, and the general public. Their empirical assessment contributed to validating the model, confirming the effect of social identity on brand equity. Wear et al. (2016) focused on the brand equity of sportswear companies' sponsorship and postulated that students' identification with a university and a sport team is associated with multi-dimensional brand equity, which consists of perceived quality, brand awareness, and brand loyalty. The results lend a counterintuitive finding; both team identification and university identification are not statistically significant antecedents of brand equity. Thus, further testing the model in various contexts is needed in order for the relationship to be clarified, leading to the following hypothesis:

Hypothesis 3–1. Team identification is positively associated with brand equity.

Online community identification and brand equity

Despite the enormous value that an online community can yield on sport organisations in terms of enhancing its brand equity and being a communication tool (e.g. promoting a team's CSR activities), online community identification has been neglected in exploring a team's brand equity, with the relationship between online community identification and sport team brand equity yet to be explored. It is, thus, critical to state the reasons why this study considers online community identification as a determinant of brand equity. This is because identification with the online community is associated with the fact that the online community offers a space where a brand or organisation can build an ideal long-term symmetric relationship, ultimately, creating a significant positive impact on brand equity with their key public (Boyle & Magnusson, 2007), while enhancing the significantly important fan-to-fan relationships (Katz & Heere, 2015).

There are empirical studies that provide evidence in understanding more in-depth how'-community' centric identification translates to'team'centric brand equity. Jang et al. (2008) established a hypothesis that stimulating community commitment would be expected to lead to brand loyalty, which is related to the concept of brand equity. Popp and Woratschek (2017) also made a critical assumption that can support the link between community-level outcomes and brand-level outcomes. They postulated that community loyalty has an impact on brand loyalty, and positive word-of-mouth intention towards the community is associated with word-of-mouth intention towards the brand. In line with these studies, Bagozzi and Dholakia (2006) also contended that 'social identity with the brand community can contribute to the participant's identification with the brand' (p. 59). This is because extra benefits that community members might have such as a relationship with and within the community or sharing information will result in members' loyalty to the brand. Given the previously outlined fact that individual's relationships with the community consequently transform to brand-level outcomes and reinforce positive outcomes towards the brand, it is assumed that identification that is found in an online sport fan community can lead to a team's brand equity as it is part of the psychological experience of being a fan. This study examines a possible direct impact of online community identification on brand equity as an exploratory hypothesis. Taking this into consideration, the following hypothesis of this study is formed:

Hypothesis 3–2. Online community identification is positively associated with brand equity.

The mediating effect of online community identification between perceived CSR and brand equity

Individuals' identification is reported to be a significant predictor of brand equity (Wang & Tang, 2018; Watkins, 2014), as well as an outcome of an organisation's CSR activities (Morrison et al., 2018). However, Woo and Jin (2016) study reveals that perceived CSR activities can have an insignificant impact on brand equity. This counterintuitive result implies the existence of alternative factors, such as online community identification, that may mediate the relationship between perceived CSR and brand equity. While Fatma et al.

(2015) tested trust and Singh and Verma (2017) examined brand awareness, brand image, brand loyalty, and purchase intention as mediators on the link between CSR and brand equity, investigating a mediation effect of online community identification has been neglected, even though identification plays an undeniably important role in understanding sport fans. Taking this into consideration, the indirect effect of CSR perception on brand equity through sport fans' identification with the team and online community is examined, leading to the following hypotheses:

Hypothesis 4–1. Perception of a team's CSR and brand equity are mediated by fan identification.

Hypothesis 4–2. Perception of a team's CSR and brand equity are mediated by online community identification.

The conceptual framework of this study is illustrated in Figure 1.

Methodology

Sample and data collection

The fans of the South Korean Baseball Organisation's (KBO) Samsung Lions baseball club were chosen as the focus of our research. Both the Samsung Lions and the online fan community of the team represent the most famous baseball club and fan community in South Korea, having won the league eight times. The online community provides a platform for fans to communicate with other fans, share the news, discuss their team's management, share their experiences, analyse game result, and plan group activities to cheer their team. The community was established in 2006 by fans, with nearly 53,000 members and over 500,000 posts uploaded by fans as of December 2019.

Since this study focuses on sport fans' perception in an online community context, a web-based survey was deemed the most effective way for data collection. Although

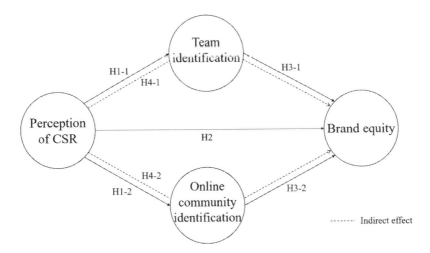

Figure 1. Conceptual framework and hypotheses.

online surveys have several inherent disadvantages such as a potential low response rate, and possible difficulties in terms of access and generating a sample from an online community (Wright, 2005), the authors were able to minimise the potential issues due to the support of the managers of the community. The questionnaire was posted on a notice board of the online fan community between 13 June 2018 and 11 July 2018, so that all members could access it. Of the 339 questionnaires collected, eight were discarded due to incomplete responses, resulting in obtaining 331 usable responses for this study.

Measurement

Multi-item scales were applied to assess each of the variables. For measuring the variables established in this research model, scales were adapted from previous studies (see Table 2 for items used). Sport fans' perceptions of CSR activities were measured using the Consumer Attitudes toward Responsible Entities in Sport (CARES) scale developed by Walker and Heere (2011). While the CARES is originally a two-dimensional scale (i.e. cognitive awareness and affective evaluation) with seven items, cognitive awareness consisting of three items was adopted in the current study. The reason for adopting the CARES scale is that it was specifically developed for the sport context. To assess the sport fans' identification with the online community, five items established by Algesheimer et al. (2005) were applied. To assess the team identification, seven items from the Sport Spectator Identification Scale developed by Wann and Branscombe (1993) were used. Measures for brand equity were adopted from Watkins (2014), who examined customer-based brand equity on the basis of the SIBE model, which underpins the causal relationship between social identity theory and brand equity in this study. See Table 2 for more information on the sample items.

Using back-translation, two academics fluent in both Korean and English translated the measurement items. Five-point Likert scales ranging from 'strongly disagree' (1) to strongly agree (5) were used for all items. Additionally, a pilot test was conducted prior to the main survey, in order to ensure its reliability and the accuracy of the expressions used. Collected data were analysed using SPSS for descriptive statistics and AMOS for structural modelling.

Results

Sample

Measurement model
Prior to examining the reliability and validity of the sample, a preliminary analysis was carried out to identify multivariate normality. The current study detects outliers based on Mahalanobis distance using SPSS 23.0 (Pallant, 2010). A total of 26 samples that had Mahalanobis distance values ranging from 22.72 to 91.34 were detected as outliers and removed for the next analysis (Table 1).

To validate the measurement model, convergent validity, discriminant validity, and reliability testing were undertaken. First, three methods were used to verify the convergent validity: standardised factor loading, average variance extracted (AVE) and

Table 1. Respondents' Demographic Profile.

Profile	Description	Responses (n = 331)	Percentage (%)
Gender	Male	217	65.6
	Female	114	34.4
Age group	18–25 years	87	26.3
	26–30 years	74	22.4
	31–39 years	102	30.8
	40 years and above	68	20.5
Occupation	Student	84	25.4
	Part-time employee	6	1.8
	Full-time employee	184	55.6
	Self-employed	11	3.3
	Retired	2	0.6
	Other	44	13.3
Highest educational qualification	High school graduate	120	36.3
	Undergraduate degree	186	56.2
	Postgraduate degree	25	7.6
Questions for sample behaviour			
How long have you been Lions' fan?	Under 1 year	7	2.1
	1–3 years	47	14.2
	4–6 years	63	19.0
	7–9 years	39	11.8
	More than 10 years	175	52.9
How many times do you attend matches for a season?	Under 1 time	9	2.7
	1–2 times	32	9.7
	3–4 times	70	21.1
	5–6 times	59	17.8
	More than 7 times	161	48.6

composite reliability (CR). Items showed standardised factor loading below .7 (C.R. > 1.965, $p < .05$) were removed, while retaining 13 items for 4 constructs that exceeded the minimum requirements as shown in Table 2 (Bagozzi & Yi, 1988). In this study, the AVE value for each of the constructs was .74, .78, .67 and .75, exceeding the recommended .5 threshold. The CR value for four constructs was ranging from .85 to .92, all of which being greater than the recommended .6 threshold (Bagozzi & Yi, 1988). Also, the reliability of the constructs was accessed based on Cronbach's alpha coefficients. With the coefficients ranging from .77 to .87, the constructs used in this study proved to have adequate reliability, exceeding the recommended .7 threshold (Anderson & Gerbing, 1988). Goodness-of-fit of the measurement model indices (CMIN/DF = 1.42, RMR = .02, GFI = .96, AGFI = .94. NFI = .95, IFI = .97, TLI = .98, CFI = .98, RMSEA = .04) reflected an excellent model fit. See Table 2 for detailed information on the validity assessments of content and the goodness-of-fit statistics.

Lastly, the discriminant validity of the constructs was accessed by comparing the AVE and the square root of correlations between constructs. Discriminant validity is a concept that compares an explanation of latent variable and observed variable with an explanation of between latent variables. If the AVE of a certain construct is greater than the square foot of the correlations between this construct and the other constructs, the discriminant validity is ensured (Hair et al., 1998). As shown in Table 3, the results showed that all square roots of the correlations between constructs were less than the AVE for each construct, therefore, achieving satisfactory discriminant validity between constructs.

Table 2. Results of Confirmatory Factor Analysis and Convergent Validity.

Constructs and measurement items (Labels)	Factor loading	Critical ratio (C.R.)	Alpha	CR	AVE
Perceived CSR			.86	.85	.74
I am aware of the social programs of my favourite team (CSR 1)	.89	–			
I know of the good things my favourite team does for the community (CSR 2)	.85	8.76***			
Team identification			.77	.91	.78
I see myself as a strong fan of the Samsung Lions? (TI 3)	.76	–			
It is important for me to being a fan of the Samsung Lions (TI 4)	.71	10.78***			
My friends see me as a strong fan of the Samsung Lions (TI 5)	.70	10.55***			
Online community identification			.87	.89	.67
I am very attached to the community (OCI 1)	.80	–			
I see myself as a part of the community (OCI 2)	.82	14.80***			
The friendship I have with other community members means a lot to me (OCI 3)	.79	14.28***			
If community members planned something, I'd think of it as something 'we' would do rather than 'they' would do (OCI 5)	.74	13.23***			
Brand equity			.82	.92	.75
I believe that overall, the team is a high quality organisation (BE 3)	.70	–			
Attending a team game is worth the time and money to do so (BE 5)	.72	10.41***			
I can recognise the team among other teams in the league (BE 6)	.71	10.12***			
I can recall the team's logo quickly (BE 7)	.72	10.24***			

*p < 0.05, **p < 0.01, ***p < 0.001
CMIN/DF = 1.42, RMR =.02, GFI =.96, AGFI =.94. NFI =.95, IFI =.97 TLI =.98, CFI =.98, RMSEA =.04

Table 3. Results of Discriminant Validity.

	Perceived CSR	Team identification	Online community identification	Brand equity
Perceived CSR	*.74*			
Team identification	.09	*.78*		
Online community identification	.14	.09	*.67*	
Brand equity	.07	.59	.06	*.75*

The italicised cells present the values of the averaged variance extracted (AVE)

Structural model and hypotheses testing

AMOS 20.0 software was used to conduct structural equation modelling in our study. The goodness of fit indices of the structural model was acceptable (CMIN/DF = 2.98, RMR = .02, GFI = .98, AGFI = .89. NFI = .94, IFL = .95, TLI = .88, CFI = .95, RMSEA = .08). The direct path linking fans' awareness of the team's CSR activities to team identification was significant (β = .25, p < 0.001), suggesting that perception of CSR is an antecedent of team identification. The direct effect from the perception of CSR to the online community identification was also found to be strongly significant (β = .33, p < 0.001), and therefore, hypothesis 1–1 and 1–2 were supported. The result showed that 11% of the total variance in community identification (R^2 = .11) and 6% of the total variance in team identification (R^2 = .06) were accounted for by fans' perceived CSR, respectively. Hypothesis 2 predicted that awareness of CSR would affect brand equity. The results indicated that the effect of perceived CSR on brand equity appeared insignificant (β = .07, p > 0.05), hence, hypothesis 2 was rejected. Hypothesis 3–1 and Hypothesis 3–2 posited that team and online community identification would lead to brand equity, respectively. The direct effect from team identification to brand equity was found to be significant (β = .56, p < 0.001), whereas online community identification was not positively associated with brand equity (β = .04, p > 0.05), and therefore failed to support Hypothesis 3–2. Dual identification and perception of CSR together explained 35% of the total variance in brand equity (R^2 = .35).

The mediation role of dual identification, team identification and online community identification, was also examined. A bootstrap procedure was used to test the statistical significance of an indirect effect and resampled 5,000 times generating a 95% bias-corrected confidence interval. The criterion for the mediation effect was judged by the exclusion of zero between the lower bound and upper bound of the confidence interval (Preacher & Hayes, 2008). For instance, the presence of zero within the lower and upper bound of the confidence interval indicates no mediation effect. Hypothesis 4–1 postulated that team identification would mediate the direct link between perceived CSR and brand equity. The result indicated that the link between perception of CSR and brand equity was fully mediated by fan's team identification (β = .14, 95% CI .08 – .21); hence, team identification can be considered a mediator between perceived CSR and brand equity. The indirect effect of awareness of CSR on brand equity through identification with the online community was insignificant (β = .01, 95% CI −.02 – .05), which does not support Hypothesis 4–2 (Table 4).

Discussion

This study examined whether the perceived CSR activities of a baseball team may relate to its brand equity, while considering whether fans' multiple identifications may mediate this relationship. The findings of our study suggest that perception of sport teams' SCR initiatives can significantly influence fans' social identity towards both the online community and the team, similarly to how perceived CSR can influence team identification according to the study of Morrison et al. (2018). This result means that a sport team can build and enhance both vertical (i.e. fan-to-team) and horizontal (i.e. fan-to-fan) relationships by focusing on the promotion of their CSR activities. With sport fans' attitudes being influenced by ethically oriented practices now more than ever, online sport fan communities can play a vital role in facilitating this CSR promotion, further assisting sport teams in strengthening vertical and horizontal relationships. Interestingly, this finding is inconsistent with previous research suggesting that CSR is not directly related to team identification, but is fully mediated by pride (Chang et al., 2016). Our findings, again, show direct

Table 4. Results of Hypotheses Test.

Hypothesis	Direct effect β (p)	Indirect effect β (CI$_{Low}$–CI$_{High}$)	Results
H1–1: Perceived CSR → Team identification	.25***		Accepted
H1–2: Perceived CSR → Online community identification	.33***		Accepted
H2: Perceived CSR → Brand equity	.07 n.s.		Rejected
H3–1: Team identification → Brand equity	.56***		Accepted
H3–2: Online community identification → Brand equity	.04 n.s.		Rejected
Proposed paths mediated by team identification			
H4–1: Perceived CSR → Brand equity		.14 (.08 –.21)	Accepted
Proposed paths mediated by online community identification			
H4–2: Perceived CSR → Brand equity		.01 (−.02 –.05)	Rejected

*p < 0.05, **p < 0.01, ***p < 0.001
Online community identification: R^2 =.11, Team identification: R^2 =.06, Brand equity: R^2 =.35

links between perceived CSR and dual identifications, which are strong predictors of positive behavioural intentions such as loyalty (Kim & Kim, 2017). In other words, the more sport fans perceive CSR, the more they identify with their team and online community. However, when it comes to the social identity-brand equity relationship, only one type of identification, team identification, had a significant impact on brand equity. Our results suggest that identification with a team was found to have a strong influence on brand equity in line with Watkins (2014) and Wang and Tang (2018) findings, showing the cause and effect between team identification and customer-based brand equity. Regarding the association between online community identification and brand equity, which was exploratively investigated, it revealed that there is no statistical evidence on the relationship. The under-researched relationship between perceived CSR and sport brand equity that was explored in this study demonstrates that, unlike Hur et al.'s (2014), Martínez and Nishiyama (2017), and Woo and Jin (2016) findings, the link between the two constructs does not exist. At the same time, identification with the team was found to be a full mediator between perceived CSR and brand equity. This implies that awareness of CSR initiatives does not lead to brand equity without sport fans' team identification, suggesting that sport fans' attitude toward their team is a prerequisite of building brand equity. Its role in influencing brand equity and being influenced by perceived CSR lend themselves in highlighting the implications of this study and underline once more the need for further research on the area.

Implications

The findings of our study offer a number of practical implications for brand management of sport organisations. First, accepting the hypothesis that perceived CSR leads to dual-identifications of sport fans, both online community and team identification, indicates that being involved in and particularly promoting a sport organisation's CSR practices can help build the online community and team identification of the fans. In terms of the association of CSR with online community identification, developing and promoting CSR can assist sport organisations in making fans feel more attached to the team's online community while increasing their sense of a shared identity, which can, in turn, influence their fan behaviour (Bhattacharya & Sen, 2003; Popp & Woratschek, 2017). In other words, by making fans aware of the CSR activities, fans become more attached to the online community, which can lead to them having a positive attitude towards the sport organisation, and thus being more loyal to both the community and the brand (Kim & Kim, 2017).In this sense, online sport fan community can be a useful communication platform for sport organisations to inform and promote their CSR practices. This implication is meaningful because sport brand managers often fail to realise the full potential of the consumer-created brand community. Brand managers have been often more focused on the marketer-created community than the consumer-created community while overlooking the fact that the consumer-created community facilitates fan-to-fan relationship building (Katz et al., 2018), which can reinforce their online community identification that has a positive long-term impact on the fan–brand relationship (Popp & Woratschek, 2017).

Identification with a team was also shown to be a robust outcome of perceived CSR. Perception of CSR activity is a form of subjective measure that allows sport fans to consider their team as a better organisation than other teams, reflecting their self-identity to the team (Morrison et al., 2018). This implies that sport teams must care not only about their success on-field but also about their social contribution activities in order to secure strong team identification of fans. Given the strong effect of perceived CSR on multiple targets of identification, being perceived as socially responsible and establishing communication strategies that can effectively promote CSR practices should be considered the sport brand managers' priority.

Another important practical implication for brand managers of professional sport teams is the uncovered mediating role of team identification in the link between perceived CSR and brand equity, which indicates that fans' team identification significantly influences brand equity in sport organisations. Unlike previous research, the current study produced counterintuitive results indicating that perceived CSR practices are not directly associated with brand equity. This study found that the effect size of team identification on brand equity is more significant than any other relationship, while there exists a full mediation effect of team identification between CSR perception and brand equity, implying that sport fans' awareness of CSR would not result in brand equity without team identification. Perceiving the CSR practices of a team may allow sport fans to feel proud of their team, reinforcing their team identification and, ultimately, enhancing the brand equity of the team (Morrison et al., 2018). This finding suggests that team identification fully elucidates how CSR initiatives lead to building brand equity, underlying its significance for brand management in sport. Indeed, the findings of our study suggest that brand managers who aim to increase the value of a sport brand must focus on building team identification, due to both its direct relationship with brand equity and its mediating role between perceived CSR and brand equity.

In terms of its theoretical implications, this study focused on a structural causal relationship among perceived CSR, brand equity and dual identification of sport fans, while underlying the dual identification's mediating effect from the sport fans' perspective. This study contributes to the sport management literature by integrating CSR and the SIBE model with the under-studied multiple identifications of sport fans; online community identification and team identification. By showing a strong predictive relationship with team identification and sport team's brand equity, the results of H_{3-1} strongly support Underwood et al.'s (2001) SIBEmodel. Although the positive effect of online community identification on brand equity was insignificant, the study expands existing knowledge by examining multiple targets, which in turns leads to another theoretical implication.

To uncover the transition from community-level outcomes to brand (team)-level outcomes, this study considered whether the online community identification is transferred to a team's brand equity. While severalstudies on brand community have proposed adding hypotheses which assume the necessity of mediators for translating community-level outcomestobrand-level outcomes (Popp & Woratschek, 2017), this study confirmed that online community identification is not directly related to brand equity which substantiates the need for the additional variable.

Limitations and future research

Despite its implications, there are of course limitations to the study. First, it involves a small sample, on a single baseball team in a single country. Although it is shown that causal claims can be made from the data through appropriate testing and the use of structural equation modelling, it follows that more longitudinal data are needed to explore the relations that are suggested in the study, while researching similar or less similar contexts. In the same vein, the sample used in this study is limited to cross-sectional data. Further studies could explore this issue while employing an experimental setting or focus group interviews which might be able to take a closer look into the synergistic effects of the interrelationships among the variables, while overcoming potential limitations that arise from the use of online surveys and self-administered questionnaires, e.g. bias and social desirability risks, correlational data.

Moreover, further research should be conducted in the emerging area of online community identification and its revealed and promising link with customer-based brand equity. Since the results of the current study indicate that promoting CSR activities through an online community and building the baseball teams' online fan community identification can be a valuable aim in marketing, it is, thus, encouraged that future research explores the area further, while studying other online communities and platforms.

Conclusion

To conclude, based on a primary data survey of the relationship between perceived CSR, online community identification, team identification, and brand equity among fans of the Samsung Lions baseball club, this study showed that the more sport fans' are aware of a team's CSR program, the more they feel connected to a team, and the more identified they feel with the team and their community. Also, brand equity can be significantly influenced by the level of team identification of fans. The former would suggest that brand management in sport should focus on promoting a socially responsible image for the brand, while the latter indicates that emphasis should be put on developing highly identified fans. Both these aspects can be considered key in increasing the value of a sport brand and thus assisting sport brand managers against the increasing pressures of today's ultra-competitive sporting world.

Disclosure statement

No potential conflict of interest was reported by the author(s).

ORCID

Argyro Elisavet Manoli http://orcid.org/0000-0001-7484-4124

References

Algesheimer, R., Dholakia, U. M., & Herrmann, A. (2005). The social influence of brand community: Evidence from European car clubs. *Journal of Marketing, 69*(3), 19–34. https://doi.org/10.1509/jmkg.69.3.19.66363

Anderson, J. C., & Gerbing, D. W. (1988). Structural equation modelling in practice: A review and recommended two-step approach. *Psychological Bulletin, 103*(3), 411–423. https://psycnet.apa.org/buy/1989-14190-001

Bagozzi, R. P., & Dholakia, U. M. (2006). Antecedents and purchase consequences of customer participation in small group brand communities. *International Journal of Research in Marketing, 23*(1), 45–61. https://doi.org/10.1016/j.ijresmar.2006.01.005

Bagozzi, R. P., & Yi, Y. (1988). On the evaluation of structural equation models. *Journal of the Academy of Marketing Science, 16*(1), 74–94. https://doi.org/10.1007/BF02723327

Bhattacharya, C. B., & Sen, S. (2003). Consumer-company identification: A framework for understanding consumers' relationships with companies. *Journal of Marketing, 67*(2), 76–88. https://doi.org/10.1509/jmkg.67.2.76.18609

Boyle, B. A., & Magnusson, P. (2007). Social identity and brand equity formation: A comparative study of collegiate sports fans. *Journal of Sport Management, 21*(4), 497–520. https://doi.org/10.1123/jsm.21.4.497

Chang, M. J., Ko, Y. J., Connaughton, D. P., & Kang, J. H. (2016). The effects of perceived CSR, pride, team identification, and regional attachment: The moderating effect of gender. *Journal of Sport & Tourism, 20*(2), 145–159. https://doi.org/10.1080/14775085.2016.1193822

Fatma, M., Rahman, Z., & Khan, I. (2015). Building company reputation and brand equity through CSR: The mediating role of trust. *International Journal of Bank Marketing, 33*(6), 840–856. https://doi.org/10.1108/IJBM-11-2014-0166

Gladden, J. M., & Milne, G. R. (1999). Examining the importance of brand equity in professional sports. *Sport Marketing Quarterly, 8*(1), 21–30. http://fitpublishing.com/content/examining-importance-brand-equity-professional-sport

Hair, J. F., Black, W. C., Babin, B. J., Anderson, R. E., & Tatham, R. L. (1998). *Multivariate data analysis*. Upper Saddle River, NJ: Prentice Hall.

Hur, W. M., Kim, H., & Woo, J. (2014). How CSR leads to corporate brand equity: Mediating mechanisms of corporate brand credibility and reputation. *Journal of Business Ethics, 125*(1), 75–86. https://doi.org/10.1007/s10551-013-1910-0

Jang, H., Olfman, L., Ko, I., Koh, J., & Kim, K. (2008). The influence of on-line brand community characteristics on community commitment and brand loyalty. *International Journal of Electronic Commerce, 12*(3), 57–80. https://doi.org/10.2753/JEC1086-4415120304

Katz, M., & Heere, B. (2015). Empowerment within brand communities: Overcoming the Achilles' Heel of scale-free networks. *Sport Management Review, 18*(3), 370–383. https://doi.org/10.1016/j.smr.2014.10.001

Katz, M., Ward, R. M., & Heere, B. (2018). Explaining attendance through the brand community triad: Integrating network theory and team identification. *Sport Management Review, 21*(2), 176–188. https://doi.org/10.1016/j.smr.2017.06.004

Kim, M. S., & Kim, H. M. (2017). The effect of online fan community attributes on the loyalty and cooperation of fan community members: The moderating role of connect hours. *Computers in Human Behavior, 68*(2), 232–243. https://doi.org/10.1016/j.chb.2016.11.031

Manoli, A. E. (2015). Promoting corporate social responsibility in the football industry. *Journal of Promotion Management, 21*(3), 335–350. https://doi.org/10.1080/10496491.2015.1021501

Manoli, A. E. (2018). Sport marketing's past, present and future. *Journal of Strategic Marketing, 26*(1), 6–18. https://doi.org/10.1080/0965254X.2018.1389492

Manoli, A. E. (2020). Brand capabilities in English Premier League clubs. *European Sport Management Quarterly, 20*(1), 30–46. https://doi.org/10.1080/16184742.2019.1693607

Martínez, P., & Nishiyama, N. (2017). Enhancing customer-based brand equity through CSR in the hospitality sector. *International Journal of Hospitality & Tourism Administration, 20*(3), 329–353. https://doi.org/10.1080/15256480.2017.1397581

Morrison, K. A., Misener, K. E., & Mock, S. E. (2018). The influence of corporate social responsibility and team identification on spectator behavior in Major Junior Hockey. *Leisure Sciences, 40*(6), 1–19. https://doi.org/10.1080/01490400.2017.1408511

Pallant, J. (2010). *SPSS survival manual*. McGraw-Hill Education.

Popp, B., & Woratschek, H. (2017). Consumer–brand identification revisited: An integrative framework of brand identification, customer satisfaction, and price image and their role for brand loyalty and word of mouth. *Journal of Brand Management, 24*(3), 250–270. https://doi.org/10.1057/s41262-017-0033-9

Preacher, K. J., & Hayes, A. F. (2008). Asymptotic and resampling strategies for assessing and comparing indirect effects in multiple mediator models. *Behavior Research Methods*, *40*(3), 879–891. https://doi.org/10.3758/BRM.40.3.879

Singh, A., & Verma, P. (2017). How CSR affects brand equity of Indian firms? *Global Business Review*, *18*(3S), 52–69. https://doi.org/10.1177/0972150917693149

Underwood, R., Bond, E., & Baer, R. (2001). Building service brands via social identity: Lessons from the sports marketplace. *Journal of Marketing Theory and Practice*, *9*(1), 1–13. https://doi.org/10.1080/10696679.2001.11501881

Walker, M., & Heere, B. (2011). Consumer attitudes toward responsible entities in sport (CARES): Scale development and model testing. *Sport Management Review*, *14*(2), 153–166. https://doi.org/10.1016/j.smr.2010.08.001

Walker, M., & Kent, A. (2009). Do fans care? Assessing the influence of corporate social responsibility on consumer attitudes in the sport industry. *Journal of Sport Management*, *23*(6), 743–769. https://doi.org/10.1123/jsm.23.6.743

Wang, M. C. H., & Tang, Y. Y. (2018). Examining the antecedents of sport team brand equity: A dual-identification perspective. *Sport Management Review*, *21*(3), 293–306. https://doi.org/10.1016/j.smr.2017.07.010

Wann, D. L., & Branscombe, N. R. (1993). Sport fans: Measuring degree of identification with their team. *International Sports Journal*, *24*(1), 1–17. https://psycnet.apa.org/record/1994-00035-001

Watkins, B. A. (2014). Revisiting the social identity–brand equity model: An application to professional sports. *Journal of Sport Management*, *28*(4), 471–480. https://doi.org/10.1123/jsm.2013-0253

Wear, H., Heere, B., & Clopton, A. (2016). Are they wearing their pride on their sleeve? Examining the impact of team and university identification upon brand equity. *Sport Marketing Quarterly*, *25*(2), 79–89. http://fitpublishing.com/articles/are-they-wearing-their-pride-their-sleeve-examining-impact-team-and-university-identity

Woo, H., & Jin, B. (2016). Culture doesn't matter? The impact of apparel companies' corporate social responsibility practices on brand equity. *Clothing and Textiles Research Journal*, *34*(1), 20–36. https://doi.org/10.1177/0887302X15610010

Wright, K. B. (2005). Researching internet-based populations: Advantages and disadvantages of online survey research, online questionnaire authoring software packages, and web survey services. *Journal of Computer-Mediated Communication*, *10*(3), JCMC1034. https://doi.org/10.1111/j.1083-6101.2005.tb00259.x

Yoshida, M., Heere, B., & Gordon, B. (2015). Predicting behavioral loyalty through community: Why other fans are more important than our own intentions, our satisfaction, and the team itself. *Journal of Sport Management*, *29*(3), 318–333. https://doi.org/10.1123/jsm.2013-0306

Strategic sport marketing in the society of the spectacle

André Richelieu and Andrew Webb

ABSTRACT
The representation of reality seems to have gained precedence over reality. In the society of the spectacle, entertainment has become the experience. Accordingly, sport organizations must increasingly provide added value to their fans' brand experience. Nowadays, entertainment and sport have merged to give birth to 'sportainment'. Through a polar type of case study, this paper examines how the strategic marketing of, and through, sport can adapt to this reality by proposing a strategic sportainment mix. This study demonstrates that the strategic sportainment mix can provide valuable insights about the theoretical fit between strategic marketing efforts by, or through, sport, on the one hand. This is in addition, on the other, to a stakeholder segmentation that categorizes fans according to their connection with sport in a society of the spectacle. The proposed sportainment mix could boost the fan lifetime value, together with both the customer and financial-based brand equity.

Introduction

Debord (1967; 1970, 2020) articulated the idea that the world is a society of the spectacle where the representation of reality has overtaken reality. This point was emphasized later by Gabriel (2012) who underscored that societies, in general, and specifically Western ones were nowadays living in the age of entertainment. Stated otherwise, 'appearance' has replaced 'being' and experience is at the center of people's lives as consumers: "Customer experience is regarded as a holistic interactive process, facilitated through cognitive and emotional clues, moderated by customer and contextual characteristics, resulting into unique and pleasurable/un-pleasurable memories (Jain et al., 2017, p. 642). It could even be said that entertainment has become the experience (Luo et al., 2020; Tandon et al., 2016), and that emotions and memories are now the commodity (Webb & Richelieu, 2021). Investigating how brands construct positive emotions is at the heart of this study.

It is in this perspective that the concept of 'gamification' appeared in the literature. Gamification consists in combining the playful aspects of a game in a non-game context by adopting gaming techniques and game-style rewards, in order to heighten customer engagement and loyalty (Hsu & Chen, 2018; Yang et al., 2017). Gamification can help

---

This article has been republished with minor changes. These changes do not impact the academic content of the article.

increase customers' commitment, their willingness to spend their disposable income and trigger a positive word-of-mouth, which can amplify the company's revenues and profits (Wolf et al., 2020).

In the strategic marketing of sport brands and the strategic marketing through sport, the manifestation of the above transformations is captured by the merger of sport and entertainment. This fusion is called 'sportainment' (Desbordes & Richelieu, 2019; Jurisport, 2013; Richelieu, 2021; Van Laethem, 2011). Admittedly, the notion of coupling sport with entertainment is not a novel idea. It was applied during the Ancient Olympics when Games were considered entertainment for the Gods, in honor of the latter (Waterfield, 2018). Besides, in the Roman Empire, the prevalence of entertainment led to the maxim 'bread and circuses' (Bell, 2020). Yet, the conceptualization of sportainment is rather recent. As such, theorizing sportainment is an ongoing endeavor: it requires a better understanding of the impacts of this emerging reality of the strategic marketing by and through sport. Examining an extreme, or polar case (Eisenhardt, 2021), is a promising approach for such theorization efforts.

Surely, the experience of sport fans has gradually been strengthened over the years by sport organizations, with co-creation being a key focus point (Kolyperas et al., 2019). In fact, even before the pandemic of Covid-19, sport managers and industry leaders were working to reimagine how to engage their fans in compelling and innovative ways, for example, via fitness apps (Tu et al., 2019), gamified programs (Hwang & Choi, 2020), not to forget virtual and augmented reality initiatives (Rogers et al., 2017; Uhm et al., 2020). Truly, all of the latter actions have accelerated with physical distancing measures being implemented by governments to slow down the transmission of the virus (Inagaki & Lewis, 2020). Covid-19 has compounded the effects of the 'tech-celeration' that was already under way (Standage, 2020). This is notwithstanding the rise of esports and its different platforms which act simultaneously as gaming sites and social media networks, a subdomain valued at over US$1 billion (Scholz, 2020).

Hence, the aim of this paper is to propose an approach for considering the complex relationships, constructed in a society of the spectacle, between brands, the sport enterprises they interact with and their stakeholders. As such, this article shall conceptualize a strategic sportainment mix through the levers of one of FC Barcelona's associated entities, the Barça Foundation and its unique museum highlighting the club's initiatives pertaining to Sport for Development and Peace (SDP). In all respects, how can a sport organization nurture its brand through sportainment by crystallizing the emotional bond with its audience? One promising answer to this question lies in understanding the fit between the sportainment level of an initiative and the targeted audience. In the spirit of the society of the spectacle, the targeted audience should perhaps be understood through different approaches than classical marketing segments. We posit that the audience should be segmented according to its relationship with sport. Effective strategic marketing of a sport brand, or marketing through sport, must present a fit between the relationship the target audience has with sport on the one hand, and the sportainment level of the sport-related initiative, on the other. In order to elaborate our proposition, the article shall follow this structure: first, a review of the literature; second, the methods; third, the case of the FC Barcelona museum, alongside our findings; and fourth, a discussion, conclusion, limitations and future research directions.

Literature review

Debord and the society of the spectacle

According to Debord (2020), life is a succession of spectacles. Social life can be interpreted as having transitioned from 'being' into 'having', and from 'having' into 'appearing'. A passive identification with the spectacle replaces genuine activity and, as a result, the rise in artificial spectacles decreases contact with reality, while simultaneously instituting the new reality and normalcy (Webb & Richelieu, 2021). The society of the spectacle lays out a society of images under new forms of political power and social organizations (Fearnley, 2019). In effect, for Debord (1967; 1970), the lack of authenticity of the society of the spectacle alters the perception people have of the reality. Debord invites people to reflect on the potential excesses of the society of consumption and how far this society has gone in selling an experience. A society where the spectacle (or entertainment; Stratton, 2021) has become the experience in and of itself, from service industries to consumer goods, and from brands in general to sport ones in particular.

In this vein, Paché (2020) points out that sport, and football more particularly, is, nowadays, a key component of the society of the spectacle, its ecosystem, as well as the source of its possible excesses. Within this environment, different stakeholders, such as federations, leagues, clubs, players, host cities and countries, participate in the staging of sporting events (from regular championship games to the Olympics and the FIFA World Cup), monopolizing significant non-renewable resources. Meanwhile, the masses are entertained and invited to consume as much as possible. If the 2022 Qatar World Cup comes to mind, as exemplified by Paché (2020), this situation of resource misallocation and avid consumption was all too well exacerbated during Covid-19 and the related sanitary crisis. Precisely, professional sport leagues around the world did everything, at the height of the pandemic, to push through the continuation of their operations, trying to salvage at all costs their lucrative TV right and sponsorship deals, taking over medical supplies, such as testing kits, at a time of significant shortage for the general public. In the meantime, fans were invited to cheer at a distance by using remote assistance applications to recreate the in-stadium experience[1],[2].

Following up on this discussion under the prism of Debord, Gabriel (2012) highlighted that in modern societies, life is displayed as an infinite series of spectacles, or entertainment; this could be even more magnified in a digital world. As people are portrayed by Debord, 1967; 1970) to believe what they are seeing and by Gabriel (2012) as consumers of an accumulation of spectacles, it is relevant to continue analyzing what insight the actual version of sport is conveying. This brings the reflection to the concept of gamification, including its ethical aspects.

Gamification

Gamification is a form of persuasive marketing. As underlined in the introductory remarks to this paper, gamification incorporates gaming techniques and game-style rewards in order to bolster customer engagement, loyalty and 'brand love' (Hsu & Chen, 2018; Yang et al., 2017). This regularly occurs via a process of co-creation with the consumer who is lured by the promise of an unparalleled engaging experience (Huotari & Hamari, 2017; Thorpe & Roper, 2019).

As a result, gamification can insidiously trigger a deep and spiraling engagement from consumers who can end up contracting an addictive or obsessive relationship with the product, service or brand (Lundahl, 2021). This is because consumers gradually find themselves unable to disconnect from the pace of the game experience or discern the blurring of the lines between the game and the product, service or brand that is associated with the gamified experience (Thorpe & Roper, 2019).

In sport, this gamification is present in physical activity and spectacle sports. First, for exercise, examples include fitness apps which can help consumers persevere in their training program when the app is made social, enabling people to interact with a community of work-out enthusiasts, besides heightening emotional value (Tu et al., 2019). These fitness apps can incorporate achievement-related game functions which can meet the participants' needs for competence, autonomy and relatedness (Bitrian et al., 2020). In addition, wearable fitness technology, which is used by health and fitness clubs to engage with their consumers, can strengthen the emotional bond with customers and foster brand loyalty (Pizzo et al., 2021). For Polo-Peña et al. (2021), gamification can be effective in encouraging users to exercise regularly, by using wearables such as smart bands or by participating in live and on-demand workouts, such as Peloton bikes.

Second, in traditional sports, gamification cases encompass mobile and digital applications, with sport event spectators enriching their experience through the integration of smartphone-enabled digital resources: by interacting with mobile and digital apps, fans can potentially become co-creators (or 'fan-actors'; Desbordes & Richelieu, 2019) of their experience and, as a result, be more engaged (Horbel et al., 2021). Yan et al. (2019) stressed the importance of social media as a potentially strategic communication resource in recognizing and legitimizing sport organizations and brands, while studying the case of Twitter at the 2017 UEFA Champions League Final. On this subject, Naraine et al. (2019) headline the prevalence of social media among Millennial users and how sport organizations can trigger synergies via cross-platform engagement (Facebook, LinkedIn, and Instagram to interact on Twitter) to engage with their brand communities and entertain them. These characteristics must therefore be taken into consideration when designing strategic marketing initiatives. Truly, the sport industry has experienced significant technological changes in its environment (Naraine, 2019a) and entertainment is a key factor in attracting fans to events held at stadiums (Mazzei et al., 2020).

Consequently, sport organizations have acknowledged the experiential value of gamification (Leclercq et al., 2020). This happens in concert with the capability of co-creation which empowers fans, while covertly inviting the latter to escalate both their commitment and involvement towards the sport brand, to the point of a stronger loyalty and higher Fan Lifetime Value (FLV; the amount of money a fan dedicates to his/her brand during his/her lifetime; Van Laethem, 2011). Therefore, some authors question the ethics of gamification: Thorpe and Roper (2019) go as far as to refer to gamification as a manipulative tactic to elicit consumer engagement and consumption without much consideration for ethical responsibility.

Sportainment and Schumpeter's creative destruction

At this moment, we could posit that the mutations that have occurred in society, alongside the changes in people's behavior and consumption, represent some major forces that impact industries, in general, and notably the sport industry. Indeed, sport has seen the consecration of sportainment: a gradual historical fusion of sport and entertainment.

What is more, Parent et al. (2018) postulate that a 'new era' of sport came into sight following, among others, technological advancements, new legislation and economic austerity. These environmental changes impact both traditional (athletes) and non-traditional stakeholders (social media), and how sport organizations are operating for the greater good via social causes (Webb & Richelieu, 2015, 2021). Moreover, as postulated by Richelieu (2021), technological developments, consumer behavior changes and stakeholders' innovations are leading to mutations that are reconfiguring sport into sportainment; with traditional and non-traditional actors driving these permutations, as it shall be explained and illustrated in Figure 1. Sport has, consequently, been gravitating further towards a sportainment model.

Unmistakably, the boundaries of sport have expanded (Funk, 2017). Sport is more than just a game: it is also entertainment for the masses, showcased at the Colosseum and Circus Maximus during the period of the Roman Empire (Minowa & Witkowski, 2012), and in multipurpose arenas around the world in modern times (Desbordes & Richelieu, 2019; Mazzei et al., 2020). In like manner, sport is a political tool that was employed, for instance, during the Cold War between the American and Soviet blocs to assert their respective political prominence (Brownell & Besnier, 2019).[3] Today, countries such as China, Qatar

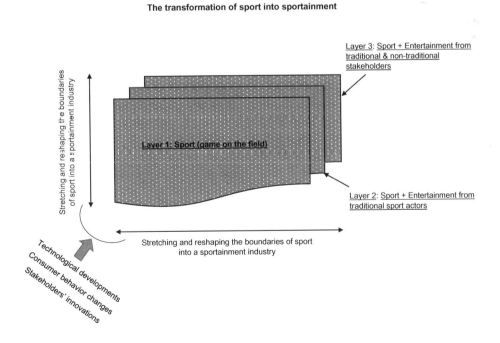

Figure 1. The transformation of sport into sportainment. Source: Adapted from Richelieu, 2021, p. 412.

and Russia, among others (Brannagan & Giulianotti, 2018; Giulianotti, 2015; Müller, 2017), aim to capitalize on sport in order to build or warrant their 'soft power': they intend on improving their image and reputation, and increasing their influence, regionally and/or internationally (Abdi et al., 2019), by virtue of a sport-oriented place branding strategy (Richelieu, 2018). It should be noted as well that sport can benefit societies at large: sport is a form of leisure that can be leveraged by marketers to create a positive impact on society. Lim (2019, p. 260) assessed that 'sports can act as an entry point to, a promoter of, an educator of, a symbol of, an initiator of conversations and dialogs on, and a unifying mechanism for national unity', all the more so in the context of a multicultural society.

Sportainment could, hence, be viewed as a natural manifestation of the society of the spectacle for its entertainment component. On the one hand, sportainment represents a process that is remodeling the boundaries of the industry where the marketing of a unique set of experiences becomes the catalyst that helps promote a sport brand (Desbordes & Richelieu, 2019; Richelieu, 2021). Thus, the sporting event becomes scripted in a theatrical way, with both sport and entertainment being knitted. In this vein, sportainment can be described as the state in which the industry is being reinvented, as sport incorporates more and more entertainment (Jurisport, 2013). On the other hand, sportainment is a potential strategic leverage for sport organizations and stakeholders alike who can, to that end, trigger an added-value brand experience for fans (Van Laethem, 2011), as it shall be embodied in the examples below.

Additionally, because of the transformations that surround the sport industry and their impact on consumers, sportainment could be linked to Schumpeter's creative destruction theory (Schumpeter, 1994). Here, sportainment can be conceived as a process of evolution that radically reshapes the structure of an industry, by dismantling the older version of that industry to create a new one, through innovations, business cycles and major shocks. On the latter, the Covid-19 pandemic would be an example of these kinds of shocks, as it emerges as a major accelerator of pre-existing trends and changes in the industry and consumption patterns. According to Schumpeter, 1994 innovations are paramount because companies that innovate contribute to the expansion of the market, weaken less innovative companies and, therefore, gain a competitive advantage over their rivals.

Figure 1 depicts how the boundaries of sport have been stretched and reshaped into sportainment. From 'Sport' (game on the field; Layer 1), the industry moved towards Layer 2 ('Sport + Entertainment with traditional sport actors'). In Layer 3 ('Sport + Entertainment from traditional and non-traditional stakeholders'), historical unconventional actors are trying to benefit from their collaboration with sport. For this reason, the creative destruction in sport is instigated by both traditional and non-traditional stakeholders (Richelieu, 2021). Traditional stakeholders encompass sport teams, leagues, federations, athletes and fans; non-traditional actors consist of artists, celebrities, entertainment companies, software firms, movie corporations, esports enterprises, poker tournaments, even politicians, and other eclectic actors.[4]

Within this paradigm, the case of the collaboration between the NBA and Take-Two Interactive, an American video game enterprise, which led to the launch of the esports NBA 2 K League in 2018, comes to mind. Through their partnerships with esports, sport properties can enlarge their customer base with gaming platforms that also act as social networks; but also fortify the emotional attachment with their current fans by diversifying their brand offering (Richelieu, 2021). Stated differently, sportainment becomes an opportunity to build bridges with both traditional sport and supporters, as well as with highly engaged, captivated, video game players and fans who now gain from high-speed streaming capabilities and immersive gadgets, as epitomized by virtual reality headsets (Inagaki & Lewis, 2020; Rogers et al., 2017). This is in line with Bertschy et al. (2020). These authors demonstrated that, when extending the brand via esports, managers should implement activities that can connect traditional sport and esports in order to make fan communities from both types of sport experience the essence of the brand. With this idea in mind, a convergence of video games, cinema, music and sport via social network platforms could manifest itself in the future (Betzler & Leuschen, 2021; Crawford et al., 2019). Thus, one of the aims of this paper is to provide insights about the theoretical limits of this convergence.

As exposed by Uhm et al. (2020), a cognitive engagement deepens the sense of presence in a virtual reality; and an increase in the sense of presence positively impacts the attitudes towards the respective sport. In point of fact, non-traditional stakeholders could be classified as 'disruptors' (Christensen et al., 2015) of the sport industry ecosystem, emphasizing in the process the transition towards sportainment and the enlargement of the latter. Nietzsche, who inspired Schumpeter's work, did outline that 'we have to learn to think differently ... to feel differently' (Weiner, 2020): this is what sportainment brings to the rationale and narrative of the sport industry nowadays.

In summary, technological developments, consumer behavior changes and stakeholders' innovations have induced mutations that have contributed to the transformation of sport into sportainment (Figure 1). Sportainment can help engage customers, entertain them, develop a bond of trust and convey an unparalleled experience to fans. It can also allow a brand to preserve its audience and acquire a new one, even revamp itself in the process. However, for sportainment to be effective, it should exhale authenticity: the sport brand must stay true to itself and its target segments (Van Laethem, 2011). At this time, we shall transition to the methods and the case of the Barça museum.

Methods

The constructs discussed so far directly influenced our decision to select a case study methodology (Eisenhardt, 1989). The 'Eisenhardt method' was retained as a roadmap for our theory building efforts because its impact on business research is substantial (Ravenswood, 2011). Building on Weick's (1996) recommendation that administrative sciences should focus on conceptual relationships, we proceeded to select a case that would provide insights into the connections between strategic marketing of sport brands, the society of the spectacle and sportainment. In other words, how do the three layers of sportainment described in Figure 1 affect strategic marketing decisions by and through sport?

Overall, our research design followed the eight steps set out in Eisenhardt's (1989) process for building theory from case study research. Details of each step may be found in Appendix A. Yet, as a case study research is an approach 'that focuses on understanding the dynamics present within a single setting' (Eisenhardt, 1989, p. 534), certain limits had to be fixed. We therefore concentrated on one element of the fan experience that is, to our knowledge, unique in the world: The Barça Foundation Museum. Launched in 1994, the Barça Foundation is a non-profit agency associated with FC Barcelona that contributes to tackling the United Nations (UN) sustainable development goals. It operates sport for development and peace (SDP) initiatives in 53 countries, reaching over 1 million children and youth worldwide. Hence, as this museum represents a unique phenomenon, the research at hand can be classified as a 'polar type' of case study (Eisenhardt, 2021): our object of research provides an extreme example of the extent sport brands are prepared to go and build relationships with their fans. This approach is pertinent, as understanding an extreme exemplar of a construct may help theorizing and generalization research efforts (Eisenhardt, 2021).

Following Eisenhardt's (1989) recommendations, multiple data collection methods were retained. These included the analysis of publicly available written assets,[5] together with digital and electronic assets presented on both the FC Barcelona and Barça foundation publicly accessible websites.[6] Third, in the spring of 2018, one of the authors conducted field work at Camp Nou by attending a United Nations SDP conference held at the team stadium which involved in-depth interviews with key Barça managers; as well as a two-hour field observation on location at the Barça Museum, thus complementing secondary with primary data.

Building on this material, the data analysis allowed us to gain an appreciation for context, exposed key messages and audiences, besides suggesting theoretical angles that could be pursued, while challenging the first outlook of the situation (Eisenhardt, 1989). The data was initially analyzed with the intention of identifying and collating representations of the three layers of sportainment.

Previous strategic sport marketing research also provided insight regarding cluster analysis (Ross, 2007). This process invites the analyst to collate persons and object according to similarities. Borrowing a more targeted approach than other sport marketing research that established broad clusters based on behavior and demographics (Narraine, 2019b), the initial clusters were extracted from the actors identified through all the analyzed data (written and electronic media, field observations and interviews). For the purposes of this study, actors were acknowledged as such, based on Latour's (2007) definition of a human or non-human entity that activates others into a given program. Subsequently, actors were further segmented according to the archetypical roles they play in the Barça narratives (Webb, 2019).

Nevertheless, as we proceeded with the analysis, other clusters of themes and new ideas about potential fan segmentation, which Ross (2007) asserts as being the primary use of the cluster analysis, inductively emerged: they led to the conceptualization of what was labelled as a strategic sportainment mix that will be presented in the discussion section. This approach helped understand the importance of the fit between layers of sportainment and a new stakeholder segmentation extracted from Debord's (1967; 1970) conception of the society of the spectacle. Stakeholder segmentations that build on the society of the spectacle and categories of the audience, according to their relationship with sport, will form the core of the discussion section of this study. First, let us present the findings.

Findings

In the highly competitive field of sport marketing, brands will go to great lengths to forge bonds with their fans. The case under study here provides valuable perspectives as to just how creative they can get. Granted, most brands leverage some forms of entertainment and games to build emotional ties with their fans. The same can be said about their cause-related marketing efforts aimed at giving back to, and forging bonds with, their communities (Ma & Kaplanidou, 2021; Roy & Graeff, 2003). This case is all the more fascinating as it is, to our knowledge, the unique example of the combined use of museum staging and education/entertainment technology that is leveraged to highlight the win-win relationships brands attempt to build through social marketing efforts (Pharr & Lough, 2012), the communication of their socially responsible initiatives (Walker et al., 2010), or by cause-related marketing (McGlone & Martin, 2006). In a sense, this case represents an utmost example of the extent to which sport brands will go to activate and solidify their fan base.

From the analysis of the data collated for this study, we found abundant examples of the three layers of sportainment. As per the first layer, namely sport on the field, it was worth observing that the Barça foundation places great emphasis on its own operations, rather than on the activities of the FC Barcelona football club. As such, most of their communication efforts and assets could be categorized in the first layer of sportainment (sport on the field; Figure 1). For instance, the first image presented in the Barça Foundation 2016–2021 strategic plan illustrates six children and a coach playing their flagship FutbolNet program that promotes inclusion and coexistence through sport. The images of children playing FutbolNet or participating in other Barça activities is also front and center at the Barça museum, as they display large pictures of both boys and girls wearing Barça bibs on the outside of the museum and in multiple locations throughout the museum. Children playing also appears on the covers of their annual reports and throughout their written assets. In short, in the collated data, images and references to children and youth, of both sexes and of different origins, playing sport are what is showcased the most frequently by the Barça.

Nonetheless, traditional sport-related entertainment (Layer 2) is also present in their operations: past and current players of FC Barcelona are commonly leveraged in their assets. For example, on their website homepage, visitors are greeted with their objective stated as 'we support vulnerable children and young people through sport and the teaching of values'.[7] Just above this statement on their landing page, an image of their new operations in New York City, is presented. By following the 'more information' link, we are introduced to their partnership with the NYC Department of education that allows them to reach 850 students, half of which have special needs. After a video about their NYC activities, the next links offer videos of players such as Sergio Fernandez, Aitor Egurrola and Ivan Rakitic interacting with children. Thus, the mobilization of athletes for social causes is a long-standing tradition for sport brands and can be linked to the second layer of sportainment (traditional sport-related entertainment; Figure 1). However, the players are seldom leveraged in the annual reports, contrary to the club's visual identity. Still, in the museum, two large images of players are featured outside the main door, along with the logo of the team in several key locations.

Evidence of Layer 3, with non-traditional sport entertainment (Figure 1), was more common in the Barça museum and on their website than in their written assets. For instance, in the museum, guests are greeted by a robot call Dream-E that explains the mission of the Barça foundation, discusses Barça activities and thanks their sponsors and partners. The next zone in the museum offers a counter where guests can play basic computer games that promote Barça values. This section is followed by a virtual reality wall where guests can wear virtual reality goggles to immerse themselves in the life of three different beneficiary children located in faraway locations, such as Colombia. Examples of the Layer 3 of sportainment are also to be found in the video capsules available on the website: a stylish video from their main partner in NYC, Thom Browne,[8] which leads to the Thom Browne FC Barcelona (FCB) fashion collection where customers can purchase FCB inspired fashion at premium prices.

Discussion

Theoretical implications

In the analyzed data, not only did we find evidence of the three sportainment layers presented in Figure 1, but we also noted that different types of actors and stakeholders were included. Indeed, athletes (both amateurs and professionals), volunteers, fans and even some spectators where all represented in the Barça museum, conjointly with the written and electronic platforms. This identification of different types of stakeholders led us to reconsider Debord, 1967 who advances that representation and appearing have replaced 'having', and that 'having' has replaced 'being' in the priorities of most people. This decline, or shift, speaks to a translation of priorities. Yet, unpacking this translation suggests that this process happens over time. As such, individuals could be laid out, at a given moment, on a specific spot of a spectrum that captures the degree to which the person values being an athlete, on one end of the spectrum, or as appearing as a fan, on the other. What is more, placing an individual actor on such a spectrum suggests that this positioning should be in relation with another construct. In other words, what does the actor try to be, have or appear to be? Conceptualizing a stakeholder's relationship with sport (re)presents the shift, translation or, in Debord's words, the decline from:

- **Being** an athlete, (labelled as **athlete**) to ...
- **Having** a favorite sport, team or athletes, (labelled as a **sport fan**) to ...
- **Appearing** to be a fan (labelled as a **spectator** who primarily consumes the entertainment offered by non-traditional sport actors and ancillary events in the context of gamification).

By segmenting audiences according to their connection with sport in a society of the spectacle, and in relation with the sportainment layers (Figure 1), it becomes possible to articulate a new way of considering strategic marketing by, and through, sport. As crystalized in Figure 2, considering the relationship a targeted stakeholder has with sport in relation with sportainment layers can then be used to better assess the fit between a sport-related marketing effort and a given stakeholder segmentation. Figure 2 allows to conceptually position the three stakeholder segmentations in accordance with their relationship with sportainment. Besides, what is labelled as a sportainment mix could be designed as a holistic framework on how the marketing mix can be reconfigured and combined with a strategic brand management (Lahtinen et al., 2020; Lim et al., 2020; Lim, 2021). In this perspective, sport managers should strike a balance between the product on the field, the classical marketing mix ('4 Ps') and brand strategies ('traditional' and digital ones, as expressed in this manuscript: Horbel et al.,

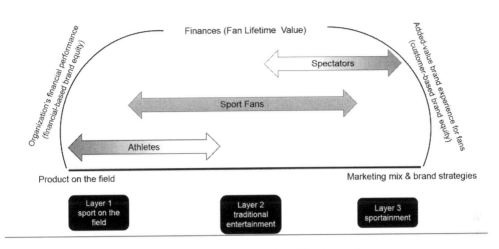

Figure 2. The Strategic Sportainment Mix. Source: Developed by the authors.

2021; Lehnert et al., 2020; Naraine, 2019a), together with the finances of the organization. It is this balance that shall enable sport enterprises to boost the Fan Lifetime Value (Van Laethem, 2011), maximize their financial performance (and as a corollary, the financial-based brand equity), in conjunction with an added-value brand experience for fans (customer-based brand equity; Figure 2).

Managerial implications

Moreover, Figure 2 demonstrates that each sportainment layer has a certain relevance with the different stakeholder segments. Based on the analyzed data, individuals who are primarily interested in participating in a sport, labelled as being an athlete, will arguably be more attracted to the sport on the field, and to a lesser degree to the activities of Layer 2. Individuals categorized as sport fans will conceivably be more interested in all three layers. Finally, spectators, or consumers who are primarily driven by entertainment and gamification, alongside artists, celebrities and even politicians (Figure 1), will plausibly only connect with the activities of Layer 3, with perhaps some interest in the activities of Layer 2 (Figure 2).

Understanding this fit is important because it allows strategic marketing to better reach a market segment; and potentially strengthen the emotional bond with stakeholders through a targeted strategic marketing mix and increase the Fan Lifetime Value (FLV; Van Laethem, 2011) introduced earlier. For instance, if strategic marketing efforts are designed to reach athletes who actively practice a sport, it is unlikely that a museum that celebrates the contributions of sport to development and peace, with a robot greeter, a virtual reality wall or a game counter, will effectively capture their attention. Rather, individuals who focus on being an athlete might prefer having an opportunity to play with disenfranchised children, coach football to youth, or participate in a FutbolNet initiative with Barça children. Whereas, at the other end of the spectrum, the casual visitor of Camp Nou categorized as a 'spectator' might greatly enjoy the game counter and the dream-E greeter robot, as they might not be very much interested in the nuances between FutbolNet and regular soccer. As they have been entertained by the museum and the gamification of Sport for Development and Peace (SDP), they could still leave the site having acquired some appreciation for the ability of sport to reduce violence or increase inclusion. Thus, the fit between the layer of the sportainment offering, and the targeted stakeholder segment appears as an important concept in the design of any strategic marketing effort by, or through, sport. That is why the strategic sportainment mix (Figure 2) could prove to be so valuable, not only for analyzing the experience at the FC Barcelona's museum; but also for other stadium museums where gamification takes center stage in order to foster customer engagement, loyalty and even 'brand love' (Hsu & Chen, 2018; Yang et al., 2017). This is notwithstanding a brand experience with an added-value for fans (Huotari & Hamari, 2017), as much as through the extensive corporate social responsibility efforts that brands deploy (Ma & Kaplanidou, 2021).

Furthermore, these stadium museums, which have sprung around the world in recent years, could reach another dimension in terms of gamification, following the acceleration of digitalization because of the Covid-19 pandemic and the inherent innovations that have accompanied this major shock. Borrowing the perspective of a Schumpeterian creative destruction (Schumpeter, 1994), sport organizations and brands that find ways to innovate could achieve two objectives: first, adapt, survive and thrive in the context of the new sportainment industry; second, as exemplified by the FC Barcelona's museum case, elaborate and implement a successful strategic segmentation that would cut across the three layers of sportainment depicted in Figure 1, while meeting the needs, wants and desires of a very eclectic mix of stakeholders who now interact within the realm of the industry. The pandemic has accelerated some changes and altered the society, in conjunction with most industries (Goldin, 2021). Innovation and the dissemination of knowledge are the cornerstones of growth for organizations and their respective industries (Aghion et al., 2021). Sportainment forces innovation but it also threatens incumbents, as the transformation of the sport industry is accompanied by the emergence of new stakeholders (non-traditional actors; Figure 1).

Conclusion, limitations, and future research directions

The contribution of this manuscript is concurrently theoretical, methodological and managerial. It comes to fruition in the strategic sportainment mix. The latter is grounded in the literature but is also brought to the fore by the case of FC Barcelona; hence helping capture the potential ramifications of the strategic sportainment mix for the actors of the sportainment ecosystem (Figure 2). This paper has underscored that sportainment has been amplified by the society of the spectacle introduced by Debord, 1967; 1970). Sportainment has also been crystallized by the notion of life as entertainment (Gabriel, 2012) and the concept of gamification where an engaging, usually co-created, experience is intended to spark more consumption, as outlined previously (Thorpe & Roper, 2019; Wolf et al., 2020).

As in all research, this project has certain limits. The first limit is that it focused on one single setting related to FC Barcelona. Truly, this is factually a polar type of case study.

Admittedly, a broader perspective that encompasses other types of sport enterprises, other forms of sport-related entertainment, or specific forms of strategic sport marketing would be beneficial in future endeavors. As it was previously stated, gamification has taken an increasing role in how organizations promise to deliver a unique brand experience to customers (Huotari & Hamari, 2017).

If this case study methodology was arguably a pertinent approach for this exploratory work, expanding the data collection methods would clearly be beneficial. Marketing managers who leverage sport to achieve their strategic objectives would, then, provide rich and nuanced perspectives. Similarly, stakeholders categorized as athletes, sport fans and spectators could also contribute to ongoing discussions about the fit between their interests and the three layers of sportainment (Figures 1 and 2).

Another limit of this model is that a stakeholder's relationship with one sport will likely be different with other sports. For instance, someone might follow Canadian gridiron football as a sport fan, watch the Rugby World Cup as a spectator but practice running and skiing as a part-time athlete. More research is needed to refine and strategically exploit the key sportainment mix proposed in this paper; whilst the boundaries of sport are continuously being reshaped into sportainment because of mutations in the society, such as technological developments consumer behavior changes and stakeholders' innovations (Figure 1). In this regard, one might rightfully ask how a sport organization's brand can effectively keep a balance between sport and entertainment, while avoiding the ambush of excessive spectacle without substance (Debord, 1967; 1970; Gabriel, 2012), in what Derrida baptized the era of desire and enjoyment (Debord, 1967; 1970; Derrida, 1967 1976)? Perhaps, the strategic sportainment mix framework might just be the fitting starting point of this reflection.

Notes

1. Please, see Remote Cheerer demo: https://www.youtube.com/watch?v=VHkC-iAVr20&feature=emb_logo.
2. This is not to mention the 'national interest' exemption that the National Hockey League (NHL) was awarded to allow teams to cross the Canada–USA border during the 2021 playoffs, even though the latter was still closed to the common citizen. In fairness, fans were gradually allowed in arenas in the spring/summer 2021, as vaccination rates started to increase
3. The 'Miracle on Ice' gold medal conquest, accomplished by the American ice hockey team at the 1980 Lake Placid Olympics, comes to mind; not to forget the boycott of the 1980 Moscow Summer Olympiad by most of the Western bloc; this was followed by a boycott of the 1984 Los Angeles Summer Games, this time by a vast majority of the Warsaw Pact members.
4. In Orlando, gaming companies are collaborating with Walt Disney, Universal Studios, sport properties and even Nasa to produce a Layer 3-type of sportainment experience.
5. Such as the 299-page 2016–2017 FC Barcelona annual report, the 8-page 2015–2021 FC Barcelona strategic plan for contextual information, alongside all currently available Barça Foundation annual reports and their 2016–2021 strategic plan (328 pages).
6. Please, see https://www.fcbarcelona.com/en/club/organisation-and-strategic-plan/commissions-and-bodies/strategic-plan-2015-21.
7. Please, visit https://foundation.fcbarcelona.com/home.
8. Please, refer to the Thom Browne's official site: https://www.thombrowne.com/ca/.

Disclosure statement

No potential conflict of interest was reported by the author(s).

ORCID

André Richelieu http://orcid.org/0000-0002-1299-9232
Andrew Webb http://orcid.org/0000-0001-8042-963X

References

Abdi, K., Talebpour, M., Fullerton, J., Ranjkesh, M. J., & Nooghabi, H. J. (2019). Identifying sports diplomacy resources as soft power tools. *Place Branding and Public Diplomacy*, *15*(3), 147–155. https://doi.org/10.1057/s41254-019-00115-9

Aghion, P., Antonin, C., & Bunel, S. (2021). *The Power of Creative Destruction*. Belknap Press.

Bell, S. W. (2020). Horse Racing in Imperial Rome: Athletic Competition, Equine Performance, and Urban Spectacle. *The International Journal of the History of Sport*, *37*(3–4), 183–232. https://doi.org/10.1080/09523367.2020.1782385

Bertschy, M., Mühlbacher, H., & Desbordes, M. (2020). Esports extension of a football brand: Stakeholder co-creation in action? *European Sport Management Quarterly*, *20*(1), 47–68. https://doi.org/10.1080/16184742.2019.1689281

Betzler, D., & Leuschen, L. (2021). Digitised value chains in the creative industries: Is there a convergence of Swiss film and game production? *Creative Industries Journal*. In press. Available at: https://www.tandfonline.com/doi/full/10.1080/17510694.2020.1796440. [Accessed

Bitrian, P., Buil, I., & Catalan, S. (2020). Gamification in sport apps: The determinants of users' motivation. *European Journal of Management and Business Economics*, *29*(3), 365–381. https://doi.org/10.1108/EJMBE-09-2019-0163

Brannagan, P., & Giulianotti, R. (2018). The soft power–soft disempowerment nexus: The case of Qatar. *International Affairs*, *94*(5), 1139–1157. https://doi.org/10.1093/ia/iiy125

Brownell, S., & Besnier, N. (2019). *Value and values in global sport. Oxford Research Encyclopedias*, October. Oxford University Press. https://oxfordre.com/anthropology/view/10.1093/acrefore/9780190854584.001.0001/acrefore-9780190854584-e-19. [Accessed July 5, 2021].

Christensen, C. M., Raynor, M. E., & McDonald, R. (2015). What Is Disruptive Innovation? *Harvard Business Review*, (December), 11. Available at: https://hbr.org/2015/12/what-is-disruptive-innovation. [Accessed

Crawford, G., Muriel, D., & Conway, S. (2019). A feel for the game: Exploring gaming 'experience' through the case of sports-themed video games. *Convergence: The International Journal of Research into New Media Technologies*, *25*(5–6), 937–952. https://doi.org/10.1177/1354856518772027

Debord, G. (1967; 1970). *The Society of the Spectacle* 2020. Pattern Books.

Debord, G. (2020) [1967; 1970]. *The Society of the Spectacle*. New York, USA: Pattern Books.

Derrida, J. (1967 1976). *De la grammatologie*. Les Éditions de Minuit.

Desbordes, M., & Richelieu, A. (2019). *International Sport Marketing. Issues and Practice*. Routledge.

Eisenhardt, K. M. (1989). Building theories from case study research. *Academy of Management Review*, *14*(4), 532–550. https://doi.org/10.5465/amr.1989.4308385

Eisenhardt, K. M. (2021). What is the Eisenhardt Method, really? *Strategic Organization*, *19*(1), 147–160

Eisenhardt, K. M. (2021). What is the Eisenhardt Method, really? *Strategic Organization*, *19*(1), 147–160. https://doi.org/10.1177/1476127020982866

Fearnley, A. M. (2019). New studies of spectacle and spectatorship in the United States: An introduction. *European Journal of American Studies*, *14*(4), 1–7. https://doi.org/10.4000/ejas.15359

Funk, D. C. (2017). Introducing a sport experience design (SX) framework for sport consumer behaviour research. *Sport Management Review, 20*(2), 145–158. https://doi.org/10.1016/j.smr.2016.11.006

Gabriel, Y. (2012). A picture tells more than a thousand words. Losing the plot in the era of the image. In F.-R. Puyou, P. Quattrone, C. McLean, & N. Thrift (Eds.), *Imagining organizations. Performative imagery in business and beyond* (pp. 230–248). Routledge.

Giulianotti, R. (2015). The Beijing 2008 Olympics: Examining the interrelations of China, globalization and soft power. *European Review, 23*(2), 286–296. https://doi.org/10.1017/S1062798714000684

Goldin, I. (2021). *Rescue: From Global Crisis to a Better World*. Sceptre.

Horbel, C., Buck, C., Diel, S., Reith, R., & Walter, Y. (2021). Stadium visitors' smartphone usage and digital resource integration. *Sport, Business and Management, 11*(1), 10–27. https://doi.org/10.1108/SBM-10-2019-0099

Hsu, C.-L., & Chen, M.-C. (2018). How gamification marketing activities motivate desirable consumer behaviors: Focusing on the role of brand love. *Computers in Human Behavior, 88*(November), 121–133. https://doi.org/10.1016/j.chb.2018.06.037

Huotari, K., & Hamari, J. (2017). A definition of gamification: Anchoring gamification in the service marketing literature. *Electronic Markets, 27*(1), 21–31. https://doi.org/10.1007/s12525-015-0212-z

Hwang, J., & Choi, L. (2020). Having fun while receiving rewards? Exploration of gamification in loyalty programs for consumer loyalty. *Journal of Business Research, 106*(1), 365–376. https://doi.org/10.1016/j.jbusres.2019.01.031

Inagaki, K., & Lewis, L. (2020). *Sony ramps up VR efforts as demand for virtual events surges. Financial Times*, May 20. The Financial Times. Available at: https://www.ft.com/content/08f620d1-a433-41e6-af7c-a12335880076. [Accessed July 5, 2021].

Jain, R., Aagja, J., & Bagdare, S. (2017). Customer experience – A review and research agenda. *Journal of Service Theory and Practice, 27*(3), 642–662. https://doi.org/10.1108/JSTP-03-2015-0064

Jurisport (2013). *Le sport mis en scène. Sport Plus Conseil*, February. Available at: http://www.sportplusconseil.com/le-sport-mise-en-scene-tribune-sport-plus-conseil/. [Accessed July 5, 2021].

Kolyperas, D., Maglaras, G., & Sparks, L. (2019). Sport fans' roles in value co-creation. *European Sport Management Quarterly, 19*(2), 201–220. https://doi.org/10.1080/16184742.2018.1505925

Lahtinen, V., Dietrich, T., & Rundle-Thiele, S. (2020). Long live the marketing mix. Testing the effectiveness of the commercial marketing mix in a social marketing context. *Journal of Social Marketing, 10*(3), 357–375. https://doi.org/10.1108/JSOCM-10-2018-0122

Latour, B. (2007). *Reassembling the social: An introduction to actor-network-theory*. Oxford University Press.

Leclercq, T., Poncin, I., & Hammedi, W. (2020). Opening the black box of gameful experience: Implications for gamification process design. *Journal of Retailing and Consumer Services, 52*(1), 1 9. Available at: https://www.sciencedirect.com/science/article/pii/S0969698919300256?casa_token=c1HCk8-DWlYAAAAA:PHoFhaqRa8ep0Zz9LCAwgmPrRVhPjYL-0pMZHpYwwhcaRYWEj7KTGdphgpYBrLYzYhslCQtTew. [Accessed

Lehnert, K., Walz, A., & Christianson, R. (2020). The booming eSports market: A field day for fans, *Journal of Business Strategy, 52*(1) Available at: https://www.emerald.com/insight/content/doi/10.1108/JBS-07-2020-0159/full/html?casa_token=IRwRO3VrB10AAAAA:_6Jtt72T0ttlJsXPZlKFLOWHvDHkBNrM95gK8CSh8rv-ZXgBXCWm9sp7Bn_5NgKFvDMjUq9kxtu3liEwcxRM_gh2JD2BgoGjZW1_e5Pp2V9YZXzhNEg. [Accessed.

Lim, W. M. (2019). Spectator sports and its role in the social marketing of national unity: Insights from a multiracial country. *Journal of Leisure Research, 50*(3), 260–284. https://doi.org/10.1080/00222216.2019.1590139

Lim, W. M. (2021). *A marketing mix typology for integrated care: The 10 Ps. Journal of Strategic Marketing*. In press. Taylor & Francis. Available at: https://www.tandfonline.com/doi/full/10.1080/0965254X.2020.1775683. [Accessed July 5, 2021].

Lim, W. M., Jee, T. W. & De Run, E. C. (2020). Strategic brandmanagement for higher education institutions with graduate degree programs: Empirical insightsfrom the higher education marketing mix. *Journal of Strategic Marketing, 28*(3), 225–245.

Lundahl, O. (2021). Media framing of social media addiction in the UK and the US. *International Journal of Consumer Studies*. In press. Wiley Online Library. Available at: https://onlinelibrary.wiley.com/doi/full/10.1111/ijcs.12636. [Accessed June 23, 2021].

Luo, J. M., Lam, C. F., & Fan, D. X. F. (2020). The development of measurement scale for entertainment tourism experience: A case study in Macau. *Current Issues in Tourism*, 23(7), 852–866. https://doi.org/10.1080/13683500.2018.1556251

Ma, S., & Kaplanidou, K. (2021). How Corporate Social Responsibility and social identities lead to corporate brand equity: An evaluation in the context of sport teams as brand extensions. *Sport Marketing Quarterly*, 30(1), 16–29. https://doi.org/10.32731/SMQ.301.032021.02

Mazzei, L. C., Moraes, I. F., Carlassara, E. D. O. C., & Rocco, A. J., Jr. (2020). Football in Brazil: What brings fans/consumers to stadiums and arenas in the city of São Paulo. *International Journal of Sport Management and Marketing*, 20(3–4), 193–210. https://doi.org/10.1504/IJSMM.2020.110834

McGlone, C., & Martin, N. (2006). Nike's corporate interest lives strong: A case of cause-related marketing and leveraging. *Sport Marketing Quarterly*, 15(3), 184–188.

Minowa, Y., & Witkowski, T. H. (2012). Spectator consumption practices at the Roman games. *Journal of Historical Research in Marketing*, 4(4), 510–531. https://doi.org/10.1108/17557501211281851

Müller, M. (2017). How mega-events capture their hosts: Event seizure and the World Cup 2018 in Russia. *Urban Geography*, 38(8), 1113–1132. https://doi.org/10.1080/02723638.2015.1109951

Naraine, M. L. (2019a). The blockchain phenomenon: Conceptualizing decentralized networks and the value proposition to the sport industry. *International Journal of Sport Communication*, 12(3), 313–335. https://doi.org/10.1123/ijsc.2019-0051

Naraine, M. L., Wear, H. T., & Whitburn, D. J. (2019). User engagement from within the Twitter community of professional sport organizations. *Managing Sport and Leisure*, 24(5), 275–293. https://doi.org/10.1080/23750472.2019.1630665

Narraine, M. L. (2019b). Follower segments within and across the social media networks of major professional sport organizations. *Sport Marketing Quarterly*, 28(4), 222–233. https://doi.org/10.32731/SMQ.284.122019.04

Paché, G. (2020). Sustainability challenges in professional football: The destructiveeffects of the society of the spectacle. *Journal of Sustainable Development*, 13(1), 85–96

Parent, M. M., Naraine, M. L., & Hoye, R. (2018). A new era for governance structures and processes in Canadian national sport organizations. *Journal of Brand Management*, 32(6), 555–566.

Pharr, J. R., & Lough, N. L. (2012). Differentiation of social marketing and cause-related marketing in US professional sport. *Sport Marketing Quarterly*, 21(2), 91–103.

Pizzo, A. D., Baker, B. J., Jones, G. J., & Funk, D. C. (2021). Sport Experience Design: Wearable Fitness Technology in the Health and Fitness Industry. *Journal of Sport Management*, 35(2), 130–143. https://doi.org/10.1123/jsm.2020-0150

Polo-Peña, A. I., Frías-Jamilena, D. M., & Fernández-Ruano, M. L. (2021). Influence of gamification on perceived self-efficacy: Gender and age moderator effect. *International Journal of Sports Marketing and Sponsorship*, 22(3), 453–476. https://doi.org/10.1108/IJSMS-02-2020-0020

Ravenswood, K. (2011). Eisenhardt's impact on theory in case study research. *Journal of Business Research*, 64(7), 680–686. https://doi.org/10.1016/j.jbusres.2010.08.014

Richelieu, A. (2018). A sport-oriented place branding strategy for cities, regions and countries. *Sport, Business & Management: An International Journal*, 8(4), 354–374. https://doi.org/10.1108/SBM-02-2018-0010

Richelieu, A. (2021). From sport to 'sportainment'. The art of creating an added-value brand experience for fans. *Journal of Brand Strategy*, 9(4), 1–15. https://www.henrystewartpublications.com/jbs/v9.

Rogers, R., Strudler, K., Decker, A., & Grazulis, A. (2017). Can augmented-reality technology augment the fan experience? A model of enjoyment for sports spectators. *Journal of Sports Media*, 12(2), 25–44. https://doi.org/10.1353/jsm.2017.0009

Ross, S. D. (2007). Segmenting sport fans using brand associations: A cluster analysis. *Sport Marketing Quarterly*, 16(1), 15–24.

Roy, D. P., & Graeff, T. R. (2003). Consumer attitudes toward cause-related marketing activities in professional sports. *Sport Marketing Quarterly*, 12(3), 163–172.

Scholz, T. M. (2020). Deciphering the world of eSports. *International Journal on Media Management*, *22*(1), 1–12. https://doi.org/10.1080/14241277.2020.1757808

Schumpeter, J. A. (1994). In *Capitalism, Socialism and Democracy*. [1942]. Cognizant.

Standage, T. (2020, November 13). After the tech-celeration. In *The Economist. The World in 2021* (pp. 23). The Economist.

Stratton, J. (2021). Glam Rock and the society of the spectacle. *Contemporary British History*, *35*(2), 210–234. https://doi.org/10.1080/13619462.2020.1822819

Tandon, A., Gupta, A., & Tripathi, V. (2016). Managing shopping experience through mall attractiveness dimensions. An experience of Indian metro cities. *Asia Pacific Journal of Marketing & Logistics*, *28*(4), 634–649. https://doi.org/10.1108/APJML-08-2015-0127

Thorpe, A. S., & Roper, S. (2019). The Ethics of Gamification in a Marketing Context'. *Journal of Business Ethics*, *155*(2), 597–609. https://doi.org/10.1007/s10551-017-3501-y

Tu, R., Hsieh, P., & Feng, W. (2019). Walking for fun or for "likes"? The impacts of different gamification orientations of fitness apps on consumers' physical activities. *Sport Management Review*, *22*(5), 682–693. https://doi.org/10.1016/j.smr.2018.10.005

Uhm, J. P., Lee, H.-W., & Han, J.-W. (2020). Creating sense of presence in a virtual reality experience: Impact on neurophysiological arousal and attitude towards a winter sport. *Sport Management Review*, *23*(4), 588–600. https://doi.org/10.1016/j.smr.2019.10.003

Van Laethem, N. (2011). La marque NBA: L'excellence dans le 'sportainment'. *Le Blog de la Stratégie Marketing*, September 5. Available at: https://www.marketing-strategie.fr/2011/09/05/la-marque-nba-lexcellence-dans-le-sportainment/. [Accessed July 5, 2021].

Walker, M., Kent, A., & Vincent, J. (2010). Communicating socially responsible initiatives: An analysis of US professional teams. *Sport Marketing Quarterly*, *19*(4), 187–195.

Waterfield, R. (2018). *Olympia: The Story of the Ancient Olympic Games*. Apollo.

Webb, A. (2019). Actantial insights: Making sense of sport for development performance account management. *Journal of Global Sport Management*, *4*(4), 371–391. Available at: [Accessed July 5, 2021] 1–18 https://doi.org/10.1080/24704067.2019.1669064

Webb, A., & Richelieu, A. (2015). Sport for development and peace snakes and ladders. *Qualitative Market Research: An International Journal*, *18*(3), 278–297. https://doi.org/10.1108/QMR-01-2014-0011

Webb, A., & Richelieu, A. (2021). Seeing is believing: Special Olympics events and the society of the spectacle. In *Event Management*. In press. Emerald.

Weick, K. E. (1996). Drop your tools: An allegory for organizational studies. *Administrative Science Quarterly*, *41*(2), 301–313. https://doi.org/10.2307/2393722

Weiner, E. (2020). *The tiny Swiss town that inspired Nietzsche*. BBC, October 2. British Broadcasting Corporation. Available at: http://www.bbc.com/travel/story/20201001-the-tiny-swiss-town-that-inspired-nietzsche. [Accessed July 5, 2021].

Wolf, T., Weiger, W. H., & Hammerschmidt, M. (2020). Experiences that matter? The motivational experiences and business outcomes of gamified services. *Journal of Business Research*, *106*(1), 353–364. https://doi.org/10.1016/j.jbusres.2018.12.058

Yan, G., Watanabe, N. M., Shapiro, S. L., Naraine, M. L., & Hull, K. (2019). Unfolding the Twitter scene of the 2017 UEFA Champions League Final: Social media networks and power dynamics. *European Sport Management Quarterly*, *19*(4), 419–436. https://doi.org/10.1080/16184742.2018.1517272

Yang, Y., Asaad, Y., & Dwivedi, Y. (2017). Examining the impact of gamification on intention of engagement and brand attitude in the marketing context. *Computers in Human Behavior*, *73* (August), 459–469. https://doi.org/10.1016/j.chb.2017.03.066

Appendix A.

Table 1. The 8 steps of the 'Eisenhardt method' applied to the sportainment study.

Step	Activity
Getting Started	The research question was set as: How can a sport organization nurture its brand through sportainment by crystallizing the emotional bond with its audience? A priori constructs include the idea that sportainment is used by both commercial sport, as well as sport for development agencies (SfD), but for far different aims (Webb & Richelieu, 2021). Yet, there is a lack of insight about how SfD foundations can use sportainment and gamification theory to concurrently construct loyalty in their members, while also contributing to the brand value of their associated sport club.
Selecting Case(s)	As the aim was to identify a theoretical sampling that could provide insights about the relationships between sport brands, their associated non-profit foundations and their mutual fan-base, it was observed that: a) not all professional sport brands have associated foundations, and b) these do not all use sportainment or gamification in their strategic marketing efforts. Thus, the available dataset that met these criteria was limited. Therefore, a *polar type* case study was selected, which represents an extreme example of the studied phenomenon (Eisenhardt, 2021). Accordingly, the chosen case is, to our knowledge, the only museum in the world dedicated to sport for development. Yet, as the Barça museum is located at Camp Nou, a few hundred meters from the main FC Barcelona Museum, this one setting did provide valuable opportunities to compare the sportainment and gamification efforts of both a commercial sport brand and its association non-profit foundation.
Crafting Instruments and Protocols	Latour's actor network theory (2007) provided a method for selecting the multiple data collection methods used for this study. Specifically, the ANT perspective that everything is data was particularly pertinent as we triangulated data: from both human (managers and staff of the Barça museum) and non-human actors, such as websites, images and the physical museum layout itself, would be collated and analyzed with the ANT perspective of actors who strive to activate. Interview protocols, themes to look for in field observation, the use of signs and symbols in written, electronic and staging technologies, notwithstanding gamification theory all helped craft research instruments that would be used. Preliminary themes were identified based on sportainment and gamification theory and would serve to help focus the field work, data collection efforts and the initial analysis.
Entering the Field	The multiple data collection methods retained provided an overlap between data collection, analysis and interpretation. Previous contacts with the Barça Foundation managers established at a European Association of Sports Management conference led to an invitation to attend a United Nations conference on SfD held at Camp Nou. This conference provided the opportunity to conduct field work in situ, as well as direct observation of both the Barça and FC Barcelona Museums. Comparing the staging efforts and edutainment offerings of both museums was very insightful. Other sources of data such as official website and annual reports produced by Barça were accessed electronically.
Analyzing the Data	The rich and varied data collected for this project enabled the analysis of the case from multiple theoretical perspectives and helped move beyond the preliminary impressions. To this end, the ANT approach of investigating how actors interact and activate others was leveraged: how museum staging, games and entertainment technologies were used to connect with fans refined the original clusters and themes.
Shaping Hypothesis	The search for the 'why' behind the activation efforts and the resulting relationships that were theoretical forged (or not), with fans suggested that there was a need to construct a better definition of 'the sport fan', as different types of fans seemed to be activated with different methods.
Enfolding Literature	Comparing the findings with both the similar and conflicting literature contributed to identifying the constructs that cold help (re)present our understanding of how sportainment and gamification activate different types of fans. These constructs were leveraged to provide generalizations that can be applied to help unpack other cases and contexts.
Reaching Closure	This phase of research was concluded when we observed that new information provided limited improvements to the data set. This occurred after all written and electronic media produced by the Barça foundation was collated, and field observations of the two Museums located at Camp Nou were done and interviews with key stakeholders had been conducted.

OPEN ACCESS

Marketing of unhealthy brands during the 2018 Fédération Internationale de Football Association (FIFA) World Cup UK broadcasts – a frequency analysis

Robin Ireland#, Magdalena Muc#, Christopher Bunn and Emma Boyland

ABSTRACT
Sport mega-events including the FIFA World Cup are a central component of consumer culture. Major brands are long associated with the World Cup, with many known for unhealthy products. This study quantified visual marketing references to unhealthy brands in the UK broadcasting of the 2018 Men's World Cup. Eight matches were recorded, and all segments of the recordings were coded for marketing references to unhealthy brands using predefined criteria. A total of 1794 such marketing references were recorded, an average of 224 per broadcast and 1.2 per minute, 95.4% of which were official sponsors. The total time of exposure to unhealthy brand marketing was six hours, 30 minutes and 45 seconds, with 22.7% of the footage including at least one unhealthy brand marketing reference. The results show the World Cup is a platform for the marketing of unhealthy brands with implications for those responsible for public health and television broadcasters.

Introduction

The men's World Cup is the most widely viewed and followed sporting event globally (KPMG, 2018). FIFA (2018) estimated that 3.57 billion people watched at least some of the official broadcast coverage of the 2018 World Cup in Russia; representing over half (51.3%) of the global population aged four years and above. In the UK, the main terrestrial broadcasters (BBC and ITV) generated 255 million video views and over 52 million hours of viewing (including two million unique viewers who saw the Sweden v England quarter-final on the BBC's digital platforms). Overall, the Broadcasters' Audience Research Board BARB (2019) reported the World Cup reached 53.1 million of the UK population (all individuals aged four years and over who viewed for at least three consecutive minutes). While data on the number of children represented in these viewing figures does not appear to be publicly available, typically approximately 15% of UK audiences are children (BARB, 2019).

#Equal contributions.
 Supplemental data for this article can be accessed here
This is an Open Access article distributed under the terms of the Creative Commons Attribution License (http://creativecommons.org/licenses/by/4.0/), which permits unrestricted use, distribution, and reproduction in any medium, provided the original work is properly cited. The terms on which this article has been published allow the posting of the Accepted Manuscript in a repository by the author(s) or with their consent.

Whilst brand management in sport, and sports sponsorship, has attracted academic interest, there has been little consideration of how brands use their commercial partnerships with mega-event organisers to promote unhealthy consumption. Whilst the advertising and promotion of tobacco products in sport has largely been removed following extensive campaigning (Arnott et al., 2007) and effective national and international policies (Shibuya, 2003), sponsorship by the alcohol, gambling, fast food and sugary drinks industries remains and may even be increasing. This has raised public health concerns (Bragg et al., 2018; Carter et al., 2013; Dixon et al., 2019; Ireland et al., 2019; Kelly et al., 2010) when the leading cause of mortality in almost all countries in the world is non-communicable diseases (NCDs) (Mathers & Bonita, 2009; World Health Organisation, 2018b) with identified risk factors for NCDs being poor nutrition, physical inactivity and smoking.

This study seeks to quantify the marketing of unhealthy brands in UK broadcasts of the (FIFA, 2018) Men's World Cup football tournament. It adds to the literature concerning the commercial determinants of health in sport, illustrating how corporate marketing practices promote unhealthy consumption.

Literature review

There is a considerable literature around sport sponsorship which considers why this area of marketing has grown so considerably over the past forty years (Cornwell, 2020). Further, there are studies into the health outcomes of the marketing of food and beverages which are high in fat, salt, or sugar (HFSS). Finally, other research has explored the exposure of unhealthy brands in televised sport. Research into mega-events enables theoretical insights into the increased commodification of sport and its globalisation (Horne & Manzenreiter, 2006) and the sport, media and business alliance that has enabled this (Roche, 2006; Whannel, 2009). Bourdieu described the commercialisation of the World Cup held in France in 1998 as 'Sport visible as spectacle hides the reality of a system of actors competing over commercial stakes' (Bourdieu et al., 1999, p. 17).

Sport sponsorship and mega-events

Sport sponsorship offers more opportunities to create brand meaning and customer loyalty (Cliffe & Motion, 2005) than advertising. Theoretical frameworks assist in understanding how sport sponsorship promotes consumerism. Pracejus (2004) asserted that even without a conscious association of a sport sponsorship, consumers may transfer positive feelings about a sporting event to a sponsoring brand (the process of affect transfer). Football is an exciting and unpredictable sport providing cultural capital and evoking strong emotions providing great value to brand managers who are able to establish brand equity in building brand awareness, brand associations, perceived quality and brand loyalty through football (Manoli & Kenyon, 2019).

Social cognitive psychological models propose potential mechanisms that help to explain the marketing processes including the efficacy of marketing that draws on emotional connections and appeals (Harris et al., 2009). These models propose unconscious or automatic processes that influence consumer behaviour (Bargh 2002) and that repeated brand exposure will also increase liking of the brand (Harris et al., 2009, 2021).

There is a large body of evidence showing the association between exposure to marketing for unhealthy brands and adverse health-related outcomes, for example studies have demonstrated marketing impacts on both the antecedents of behaviour (e.g., awareness, intended consumption) and actual behaviour (use/intake) (Kelly et al., 2015) with evidence meeting the criteria for a causal relationship (Norman et al., 2016). Many studies focus on young people, for example, showing evidence of effects of food advertising exposure on children's immediate food intake as well as intermediate and long-term adverse effects on diet-related attitudes, behaviours, preferences, and health outcomes (E. Boyland et al., 2016; Buchanan et al., 2018; Dehghan, 2019; Forde et al., 2019; Kelly et al., 2015; Russell et al., 2019).

Mega-event sponsors demand exclusivity for their brands with respect to both advertising and retail sales ensuring more comprehensive exposure and higher profile (Hall, 2006). Sponsoring the World Cup enables immense brand exposure across sports venues, broadcasting and digital media (Bragg et al., 2018; Cornwell, 2020; Morgan et al., 2017; Semens, 2017) and the World Cup brand itself may enable the excitement around the tournament to be transferred to a sponsor (Bragg et al., 2018; Madrigal et al., 2005).

Bourdieu et al., 1999, p. 130) wrote of the 'continuing battles between commercial interests in sport and the anti-smoking and anti-drinking health lobby' at the World Cup held in France in 1998. Anheuser-Busch (the producer of Budweiser) lobbied the French government and the European Commission (unsuccessfully) to enable the advertising of their beer at the World Cup despite the 1991 French Evin Law banning advertisements for alcohol and tobacco at sports events. Giulianotti and Robertson (2009) conceptual analysis of football illustrates the role the sport plays in globalisation. Football's commodification and sponsorship has historically been important for transnational corporations such as Anheuser-Busch (now AB InBev) (Meenaghan, 2001) who use the World Cup to engage consumers (Karg & Lock, 2014).

Measuring the exposure of unhealthy brands in broadcast sport

To the authors' knowledge there have been few previously published studies that explore the holistic exposure of unhealthy brands (inclusive of foods and beverages, alcohol and gambling) in broadcast sport. Studies have tended to focus on one, or occasionally two, of these product categories in isolation and have often been limited in the exposure types included. For example, research into the frequency and nature of alcohol and tobacco advertising in televised sport in the US showed audiences were exposed regularly to alcohol and tobacco brands through both television commercials and stadium signage (Madden & Grube, 1994). Further studies have considered alcohol marketing in isolation in televised English club football coding all references and found extensive visual only (Adams et al., 2014) or visual and verbal references (Graham & Adams, 2014). Purves et al. (2017) used a similar approach to explore alcohol marketing at EURO2016. Outside of the UK, there is a growing literature concerning unhealthy marketing messages in sport particularly in Australia and New Zealand (Bestman et al., 2015; Carter et al., 2013; Chambers et al., 2017; Lindsay et al., 2013; Nuss et al., 2019)

To our knowledge, no academic study has considered the marketing of all unhealthy brands at a sports mega-event including all visual brand references in in-play and out-play including commercial breaks.

Methods

Design

Based on methodology used by Purves et al. (2017) and Graham and Adams (2014), a content (frequency and duration) analysis of all visual marketing references to unhealthy brands was undertaken on eight broadcasts of the FIFA World Cup 2018 tournament, as broadcast on UK television. In order to provide an illustrative overview of the level of marketing from the various commercial actors, and because of the recognition that marketing through sport typically takes a strong brand-driven approach (Dixon et al., 2019), marketing references were categorised by brand, rather than at the product level, into alcohol, gambling or food and beverages categories.

Selection of broadcasts

We coded matches broadcast by the non-commercial, public service provider BBC and the main commercial broadcaster ITV (four quarter finals, two semi-finals and two broadcasts of the final game, one from each broadcaster; TABLE 1).

The selected broadcasts were recorded in their entirety to DVD, including all pre- and post-match discussion and interviews, as well as all playing time, pundit analysis and any commercial breaks.

Defining unhealthy brand marketing references

A reference was defined as any visual reference to providers (brands) of unhealthy foods and beverages, alcohol or gambling that lasted for two seconds or longer. We considered all gambling and alcohol marketing to be inherently unhealthy. Whilst we recognise that at the product level there is more nuance for food/beverage marketing (if, for example, sugar-free products are promoted) we considered marketing for these brands to be unhealthy if their core product fell into an unhealthy category (e.g., fast food, ice cream, sugar sweetened beverages). This is consistent with evidence that advertising for healthier products from these companies does not necessarily drive healthier choice but does drive desire for that brand overall (E.J. Boyland et al., 2015) as well as potentially misleading to younger audiences (Bernhardt et al., 2014).

References were coded across all segments of the broadcast. If the camera changed shot, but the reference source remained the same this was considered the same reference. A new reference was counted if a source went out of shot for more than one second. The same appearances shown in replays were counted as new references. If more than one brand was displayed during the same camera shot, each brand was coded as a separate reference. If multiple references of the same brand appeared in the same type of location (multiple logos of the same brand on the pitch-border) they were coded as the same reference, but the number of identical references was recorded. References were only coded when they were clear and unambiguous i.e. researchers did not infer a reference from partial, blurred or obscured footage.

Table 1. Descriptive characteristics of the coded games. Length of the broadcast and times of exposure to unhealthy brand references are presented as hours, minutes and seconds (hh:mm:ss). n- Number of coded games in the stage.

Descriptive of the coded games									
Stage/Date	Teams	Date	Day of the week	Time (GMT)	Channel	Length (hh:mm:ss)	n	Time of exposure	Percent of the footage with exposure	Average no of exposures per minute
Quarter-Finals (n = 4)	Uruguay – France	06/07/2018	Friday	2.00pm	ITV	02:48:22	172	00:37:41	22.38%	1.0
	Brazil – Belgium	06/07/2018	Friday	6.00pm	BBC	02:56:50	233	00:55:06	31.16%	1.3
	Sweden – England	07/07/2018	Saturday	3.00pm	BBC	03:28:18	175	00:51:14	24.60%	0.8
	Russia – Croatia	07/07/2018	Saturday	6.00pm	ITV	04:11:31	272	00:57:58	23.05%	1.1
Semi-Finals (n = 2)	France – Belgium	10/07/2018	Tuesday	6.00pm	BBC	02:56:56	188	00:47:49	27.03%	1.1
	England – Croatia	11/07/2018	Wednesday	6.00pm	ITV	04:34:45	261	01:02:15	22.66%	0.9
Final (n = 2)	France – Croatia (BBC)	15/07/2018	Sunday	3.00pm	BBC	03:42:28	286	00:37:55	17.04%	1.3
	France – Croatia (ITV)	15/07/2018	Sunday	3.00pm	ITV	04:02:03	207	00:40:47	16.85%	0.9
TOTAL for all games						28:41:13	1794	06:30:45	22.70%	1.2

Codebook variables

All references were captured manually using a codebook that was adopted from those used in Purves et al. (2017) and Graham and Adams (2014). Variables coded for each reference were:

- Broadcast segment (e.g., pre-match, first half, half time).
- Location (e.g., pitch border, interview area, video segments).
- Format (e.g., static advertising, electronic advertising, spot advertisement).
- Duration of reference (in seconds)
- Number of identical reference visible at same time (e.g., across multiple pitch borders).
- Brand featured (e.g., McDonald's, Budweiser, William Hill).
- Category of the product (food/beverage, alcohol or gambling. Due to existing regulations (World Health Organisation, 2018a) we did not expect any tobacco references, but these would also have been recorded)
- Nature of brand reference (e.g., direct reference – such as brand names/logo – or indirect reference – no name/logo was present but the brand was identifiable from other signifiers such slogans, colours, and typefaces).

Full definitions for all codes are provided in Appendix A.

Procedure and inter-rater reliability

Recorded broadcasts were coded by MM (n = 5) and RI (n = 3). Recorded files were viewed on a PC using media player software. Data were coded in a Microsoft Excel spreadsheet with a separate spreadsheet used for each broadcast. To test inter-rater reliability (IRR), MM and RI both coded the same broadcast (ITV final). As there was no predefined total number of references in the game, we compared the number (and percentage) of coded references in total and per segment, location, format, brand and category of the game coded by one rater with numbers coded by the second rater (the higher number from the compared pair was treated as 100%). For example, MM coded a total of 207 references in the ITV final whilst RI coded 253 references. Agreement for the total number of references was therefore (207*100)/253 = 81.8%, which is considerably above the 70% threshold for acceptable agreement for all studied variables (Stemler & Tsai, 2008). The same agreement was calculated for each variable of the codebook and the detailed results are presented in Supplementary Table 1.

Ethics

Data used were obtained through publicly available sources and therefore no ethical approval was required.

Data analysis

Data were analysed using SPSS version 24 (SPSS Inc., Chicago, IL, USA) and Microsoft Excel 2016 (Microsoft Corporation, Washington, WA, USA). Duration of each reference was calculated from the start and end times recorded. In addition, due to the overlapping of some references (multiple brands appearing on the screen at the same time but coded as different reference entries) we calculated the intervals between references. That allowed us to calculate the total time of exposure to unhealthy brands per game and across all broadcasts, excluding overlaps. We calculated the percentage of the broadcast with unhealthy brand references by dividing the number of minutes containing references by the total time of the broadcast.

We calculated the total number of references and the average number of references per game and for each of the codebook variables. Similarly, we calculated the mean number of references per broadcast minute of broadcast across all games, for each game and for each of the codebook variables. The mean number of references per broadcast minute was computed by dividing the total number of references by the length of each broadcast, and then by dividing the number of references in-play and out-of-play by the respective length of each segment in the broadcast. The values were compared for the types of games coded based on the broadcasting channel (BBC, ITV), national focus (England, non-England), kick off time (afternoon, evening) and the day of the match (weekend, week-day).

Due to the positively skewed distribution of the duration of references and number of identical references we calculated means, medians and modes for these variables. For each of the brands, we calculated the frequencies and the mean number of identical items referring to the same brand visible at the same time.

To account for the difference in the bodies that control different elements of marketing present during the broadcast, we ran subgroup analysis for the pitch-border (controlled by FIFA) and commercial break (ITV only, controlled by the broad-caster) references separately. For each of these two locations, we calculated the frequencies of references by brands and categories. For pitch border we additionally calculated the mean number of identical references to the same brand visible at the same time.

Results

Across the entire sample (eight broadcasts, totalling 28 hours, 41 minutes and 13 seconds of coverage), a total of 1794 unhealthy brand marketing references were recorded, with an average of 224 per broadcast and 1.2 per broadcast minute. The total time of exposure to unhealthy brand marketing was six hours, 30 minutes and 45 seconds, with 22.7% of the footage including at least one unhealthy brand marketing reference (see TABLE 1). The median duration of the references was nine seconds.

Of all references to unhealthy brands, 74.8% (1318) were for food or beverage brands, 24.8% (437) were alcohol and 2.2% (39) were gambling. Gambling references only occurred in commercial breaks. A total of 95.4% of all references were of the main sponsors of the FIFA World Cup, namely McDonald's (n = 439, 24.9%), Budweiser (n = 416, 23.6%), Coca-Cola (n = 392, 22.2%), Mengniu[1] (n = 305, 17.0%) and Powerade (n = 160, 8.9%). See TABLE 2 for details on the distribution of references across the codebook variables.

The most common reference location was the pitch border (n = 1304, 72.7%) with brands either sharing (n = 1151, 64.2%) or having exclusive use of this space (n = 295, 16.4%). Of the pitch border references, most were food/beverage brands

Table 2. Frequencies (n and %) of references and average number (avg. no) of exposures per game presented for each category of the variables of the codebooks.

N = 1794		No of games	n	%	Avg. no of exposures across all games
Segment	1st half	8	510	28.9	64
	2nd half	8	499	28.3	62
	Commercial break	4	84	4.8	11
	Half-time	8	80	4.5	10
	Post-match	8	190	10.8	24
	Pre-match	8	324	18.4	41
	Extra time	2	84	4.8	42
	Break in extra time	2	11	0.6	6
	Penalties	1	12	0.7	12
Channel	BBC	4	882	49.2	221
	ITV	4	912	50.8	228
Location	Commercial break ad	4	84	4.7	21
	Field of play	8	59	3.3	7
	Interview area	8	105	5.9	13
	Other (specify in notes)	8	8	0.4	1
	Pitch border	8	1304	72.7	163
	Sponsorship lead in/out	4	45	2.5	11
	Stadium Interior	8	18	1.0	2
	Video segment	8	171	9.5	21
Format	Commercial spot ad	4	86	4.8	22
	Electronic advertising (all)	8	295	16.4	37
	Electronic advertising (part)	8	1151	64.2	144
	Other (specify in notes)	8	57	3.2	7
	Product or Packaging	8	40	2.2	5
	Sponsorship lead in	4	43	2.4	11
	Static advertising	8	122	6.8	15
Category	Alcohol	8	437	24.4	55
	Food/beverage	8	1318	73.5	165
	Gambling	4	39	2.2	10
Brand	McDonald's	8	439	24.5	55
	Budweiser	8	416	23.2	52
	Coca-Cola	8	392	21.9	49
	Mengniu	8	305	17.0	38
	Powerade	8	160	8.9	20
	Others	8	82	4.6	10
Type of reference	Direct	8	1730	96.4	216
	Indirect	8	64	3.6	8
In play	In play	8	1105	61.6	138
	Out of play	8	689	38.4	86
National focus	England Game	2	404	22.5	202
	non-England game	6	1358	75.7	226
Kick off	Afternoon	4	796	44.4	199.0
	Evening	4	998	55.6	249.5
Day of match	Weekday (Monday–Thursday)	4	854	47.6	213.5
	Weekend (Friday–Sunday)	4	940	52.4	235.0
Kick off	Afternoon	4	840	46.8	210
	Evening	4	922	51.4	231
Day of match	Weekday (Monday–Thursday)	4	822	45.8	206
	Weekend (Friday–Sunday)	4	940	52.4	235

(1000, 76.7%). Alcohol accounted for 23.3% (304) of all pitch border references, but no gambling marketing references were present here. In order of frequency of references the main pitch side brands were McDonald's (n = 326, 25.0%), Budweiser (n = 304, 23.3%), Coca-Cola (n = 295, 22.6%), Mengniu (n = 259, 19.9%) and Powerade (n = 120, 9.2%).

Table 3. Average number of identical exposures in one entry.

Brand	All locations (N = 1794)		Pitch border only (n = 1304)	
	N	Mean (SD)	N (%)	Mean (SD)
McDonald's	432	6.1 (3.7)	326 (25.0)	5.9 (3)
Coca-Cola	385	5.3 (3.6)	295 (22.6)	5.6 (3.7)
Mengniu	301	4.2 (2.0)	259 (19.9)	4.1 (2)
Powerade	159	3.5 (1.7)	120 (9.2)	4 (1.6)
Budweiser	406	3.4 (1.8)	304 (23.3)	3.7 (1.9)
Other	82	2.2 (2.3)	0 (0.0)	NA

Table 4. Average numbers of exposures and average numbers (no) of exposures per minute of broadcast presented per segment, in- and out of play segments and types of games. Results presented as means, standard deviations (SD) and standard errors of means (SE).

Variable	N = 1794	No of games	no of exposures Mean (SD)	SE	no of exposures per minute Mean (SD)	SE
Segment	Pre-match	8	40.5 (12.3)	4.4	0.9 (0.3)	0.1
	1st half	8	63.8 (12.9)	4.6	1.4 (0.3)	0.1
	half-time	8	10 (7.3)	2.6	0.7 (0.4)	0.2
	commercial break	4	21 (8.1)	4.1	1.4 (0.1)	0.1
	2nd half	8	62.4 (12.9)	4.5	1.3 (0.3)	0.1
	post-match	8	23.8 (10.4)	3.7	0.6 (0.3)	0.1
	extra time	2	42 (8.5)	6.0	1.1 (0.1)	0.0
	break in extra time	2	5.5 (4.9)	3.5	0.7 (0.4)	0.3
	penalties	1	12 (NA)	NA	NA	NA
Channel	BBC	4	220.5 (50.2)	25.1	1.1 (0.2)	0.1
	ITV	4	227.8 (46.6)	23.3	1.0 (0.1)	0.1
In play	In play	8	58.2 (17.4)	4.0	1.4 (0.4)	0.1
	Out of play	8	23.0 (15.4)	2.8	0.8 (0.4)	0.1
National focus	England Game	2	218 (60.8)	43.0	0.9 (0)	0.0
	non-England game	6	226.2 (45.6)	18.6	1.1 (0.2)	0.1
Kick off	Afternoon	4	199 (41.9)	21.0	1.0 (0.1)	0.1
	Evening	4	249.3 (35.9)	18.0	1.1 (0.2)	0.1
Day of match	Weekday (Monday–Thursday)	4	213.5 (40.9)	20.4	1.1 (0.2)	0.1
	Weekend (Friday–Sunday)	4	234.8 (52.5)	26.3	1.0 (0.2)	0.1

Of the 84 unhealthy marketing references in commercial breaks (accounting for less than 5% of total references in this study), gambling was the most frequent unhealthy brand category (n = 38, 45.2%). Food/beverages and alcohol accounted for 26.2% (n = 22) and 28.6% (n = 24) of these references respectively.

The number of identical references (of the same brand) on the screen varied between one and 22, with an average (mode and median) of four. McDonald's and Coca-Cola had the most identical references in one entry with 6.1 (SD = 3.7) and 5.3 (SD = 3.6) per exposure respectively (see TABLE 3).

References appeared more frequently during in-play than out of play segments (1.4 vs 0.8 references per minute). There was no difference in the average number or frequency of references per game between broadcasters. References were the most frequent during penalties (2.5 ref/min) followed by the commercial break (1.5 ref/min). They were least frequent during the out of play segments such as pre- and post-match (0.9 ref/min and 0.6 ref/min), half time (0.7 ref/min) and break in extra time (0.8 ref/min). See TABLE 4.

Discussion

This study examined the exposure of unhealthy brands at the 2018 World Cup to enable increased understanding of the globalisation and commodification of sport. It adds to the literature around how corporate practices in sport may be detrimental to population health. The World Cup enjoys huge television coverage with the valuable broadcasting rights and commercial sponsorship providing a considerable income to FIFA (Solberg & Gratton, 2014). The marketing of unhealthy brands during the 2018 FIFA Men's World Cup was frequent and extensive, with almost a quarter of the footage including one or more reference. The most common location of marketing references was the pitch-border advertisement boards. A viewer watching these matches would have been exposed to marketing of an unhealthy brand on average 1.2 times per minute with an average of 224 exposures per game. Following Bourdieu (1986), it is clear that the economic capital of transnational corporations uses the rich cultural capital and global appeal of the World Cup to market unhealthy commodities (Ireland et al., 2021).

There were two main avenues of promotion for brands during the broadcast. The in-game marketing (mainly of the official sponsors of the event and falling within the regulatory powers of FIFA) and the marketing during the out-of-game segments, regulated at the national level by the broadcasters. As a result, during the football matches themselves, food, beverage and alcohol marketing was highly visible on both channels while the commercial breaks (ITV only) were dominated by gambling brands. While both in-game and commercial break advertising present clear concerns for public health, in-game adverts make up the majority of exposures. Given that 95.4% of all exposures were to official sponsors of the World Cup, FIFA's commercial partnerships can be considered the most significant driver of these exposures. It is clear from these data that the World Cup, as with other sport mega-events like the Olympics (Roche, 2006), is a widely used vehicle for the propagation of brand imagery and messaging for some of the biggest global alcohol, food/beverage and gambling brands.

The previous UK studies which considered alcohol marketing in isolation in televised football, found extensive visual only (Adams et al., 2014) or visual and verbal references (Graham & Adams, 2014; Purves et al., 2017). Consistent with the findings of the current study, all three found the most marketing references to be at the pitch border of the playing field where sponsors' brands were displayed electronically.

Whilst it is difficult to be precise about how many young people watch sport, we know it is very popular. For example an Ofcom report (Ofcom, 2017) found that 38% of children aged 12 to 15 in the UK are interested in sport, after music and celebrities. Thus, if we take into account the potential public health issues arising from consumption and use of the unhealthy brands we assessed, the findings are deeply concerning. Further, emerging evidence suggests sport sponsorship and marketing has an adverse effect on children's consumption, preferences and attitudes including a normalisation of the association of sports with unhealthy behaviours (Bragg et al., 2018; Dixon et al., 2019; Djohari et al., 2019; Kelly et al., 2011; Nuss et al., 2019).

We argue that the promotion of unhealthy brands at the World Cup is detrimental to population health and in direct contradiction to any aspirations of corporate social responsibility. Football has a global audience with an exceptional impact on economies, society and the media. Given that emotionally-driven marketing and sponsorship has been found to be the most effective (Meenagahan & O'Sullivan, 2001), a financially driven partnership of alcohol and fast food and sugar sweetened beverage brands with the World Cup, and its ability to engage with the *passion points* of football fans together with the frequent broadcaster's marketing of gambling is likely to have resulted in a highly effective promotion of unhealthy brands to a huge audience. The repeated exposure of brands such as McDonald's, Budweiser, Powerade and Coca-Cola on digital displays on pitch perimeters are likely to make brand associations which both influence consumer behaviour and increase the liking of these brands. We can conclude that the sponsorship of the 2018 FIFA World Cup by unhealthy commodity industries is also likely to create favourable impressions of their brands and to increase consumption of their products.

Chambers and Sassi (2019) argue for more comprehensive regulation in sport sponsorship which covers all unhealthy sponsorship rather than product by product. Certainly, policy makers should turn their eyes to sport and, football – the world's most popular sport – in particular, as continuing to allow the marketing that has been described in this paper undermines existing policies designed to protect children and their health. Further, the World Health Organisation's collaboration with FIFA to 'promote healthy lifestyles through football globally' (World Health Organisation, 2019) should be reconsidered whilst FIFA allows the World Cup to be a vehicle to promote unhealthy consumption. The commodification of elite sport, as at the World Cup, demands ethical attention (Walsh & Giulianotti, 2001) when the scale of the marketing of unhealthy brands is as high as described in this study. It raises regulatory issues for national governments in dealing with the complex management and delivery of sports mega-events especially where these are the responsibility of supranational organisations such as FIFA.

Limitations

This study had many strengths but also some limitations. Our estimates represent potential viewer exposure to unhealthy brand marketing references, and not actual exposure or any effect on the viewer. Elements such as location and size of the reference, and previous familiarity with the brand among others could moderate the impact on behaviour. The coding was done manually by researchers and therefore there is potential for subjectivity and bias. Future studies should explore the potential of automated methods to identify and capture visual references to unhealthy branding. Because an average viewer is not likely to pay close or conscious attention to marketing specifically, we sought to avoid overestimation of the exposure. For example, we only included exposures of two seconds or more and did not include partial, blurred or obscured references. While some of these limitations may have affected the number of references we identified, they do not change the meaning and importance of these findings, as there is no known safe and acceptable level of exposure to unhealthy marketing. The numbers presented here are only intended to be descriptive, to highlight the scale of the problem, not to be an exhaustive account.

The study benefitted from a pre-defined codebook used in previous published work. We discussed and resolved coding queries, and where necessary, sought the advice and guidance of other researchers in the field. We cross-checked our findings and reported on coding consistency. Having considered all the matches from the quarter-finals onwards in the World Cup, we are satisfied that our sample size is appropriate to demonstrate the results shown.

Research recommendations

Given the limited studies concerning sport sponsorship and unhealthy brands, there are considerable opportunities for future research. The influence of transnational companies in promoting their corporate brands at mega-events and disregarding national regulations requires more consideration if appropriate governance mechanisms are to be proposed.

As we understand that sponsors seek to engage with fan-consumers using the cultural capital of sport to develop brand image as well as increase consumption, more studies are required to understand how effective this engagement is. This should include quantifying the impact of exposure to unhealthy brand marketing through sports on children's attitudes and behaviours.

There are also some practical research recommendations in developing methods in the measurement of brand images in broadcasting.

This study has considered the men's FIFA World Cup. As well as the study of brand management and sponsorship at mega-events, there are many other opportunities in considering the marketing of unhealthy commodities in both women's and men's sport, amateur and professional, and of course within junior sport where public health concerns may be even higher.

Conclusions

This study is the first research to examine unhealthy brand marketing at a mega-event. It highlights the significant role the World Cup plays in providing a global market and illustrates how the cultural capital of sport, including the opportunities it provides for celebration and passion, makes it an ideal vehicle for transnational corporations. The study has demonstrated that UK viewers of the 2018 FIFA Men's World Cup were exposed to a vast amount of marketing for unhealthy brands – 1.2 per broadcast minute – highlighting the central role of sport in global brand promotion. During match footage, exposure was dominated by references to unhealthy foods and drinks, alongside alcohol, 95.4% of which were official sponsors. During commercial breaks, gambling brands dominated. In the context of the challenges to global public health presented by widespread obesity, growth in non-communicable diseases and rising rates of poor mental health, regulators and policy makers should consider the impact that marketing in broadcasts of major sporting events might be having on these outcomes. Football authorities, such as FIFA, and television broadcasters also have an important role to play, and should consider the negative social value that the promotion of unhealthy brands may have on the population's health and wellbeing, and not just the financial value of the advertising it is able to sell.

Notes

1. The Mengniu Dairy company is a Chinese manufacturing and distribution company of dairy products and ice-cream.

Acknowledgments

The authors would like to acknowledge and thank Richard Purves and Nathan Critchlow for their methodological advice and support. The authors would also like to thank Essie Li for her support with brand identification and translation of Chinese text.

Disclosure statement

No potential conflict of interest was reported by the author(s).

Funding

There is no funding to declare.

Data availability statement

The data set supporting this research is available on request from the corresponding author.

References

Adams, J., Coleman, J., & White, M. (2014). Alcohol marketing in televised international football: Frequency analysis. *BMC Public Health*, *14*(1), 473. https://doi.org/10.1186/1471-2458-14-473
Arnott, D., Dockrell, M., Sandford, A., & Willmore, I. (2007). Comprehensive smoke-free legislation in England: How advocacy won the day. *Tobacco Control*, *16*(6), 423–428. https://doi.org/10.1136/tc.2007.020255
BARB (2019) *Universes, available*: https://www.barb.co.uk/resources/universes/ [accessed 8 July 2019].
Bargh, J. A. (2002). Losing consciousness: Automatic influences on consumer judgment, behavior, and motivation. *Journal of Consumer Research*, *29*(2), 280–285. https://doi.org/10.1086/341577 available
Bernhardt, A. M., Wilking, C., Gottlieb, M., Emond, J., & Sargent, J. D. (2014). Children's reactions to depictions of healthy foods in fast-food television advertisements. *JAMA Pediatr*, *168*(5), 422–426. https://doi.org/10.1001/jamapediatrics.2014.140
Bestman, A., Thomas, S., Randle, M., & Thomas, S. D. M. (2015). Children's implicit recall of junk food, alcohol and gambling sponsorship in Australian sport. *BMC Public Health*, *15*(1022), 1–9. https://doi.org/10.1186/s12889-015-2348-3
Bourdieu, P. (1986). The forms of capital. In J. E. Richardson (Ed.), *Handbook of theory of research for the sociology of education*, (pp. 241–258). Greenwood Press.
Bourdieu, P. (1999). The state, economics and sport. In H. Dauncey and G. Hare (Ed.), *France and the 1998 World Cup,the national impact of a world sporting event*,(pp. 15–21). Frank Cass

Boyland, E., Nolan, S., Kelly, B., Tudur-Smith, C., Jones, A., Halford, J., & Robinson, E. (2016). Advertising as a cue to consume: A systematic review and meta-analysis of the effects of acute exposure to unhealthy food or non-alcoholic beverage advertising on intake in children and adults. *American Journal of Clinical Nutrition, 103*(2), 519–533. http://dx.doi.org/10.3945/ajcn.115.120022 available

Boyland, E. J., Kavanagh-Safran, M., & Halford, J. C. G. (2015). Exposure to 'healthy' fast food meal bundles in television advertisements promotes liking for fast food but not healthier choices in children. *British Journal of Nutrition, 113*(6), 1012–1018. https://doi.org/10.1017/S0007114515000082

Bragg, M. A., Roberto, C. A., Harris, J. L., Brownell, K. D., & Elbel, B. (2018). Marketing food and beverages to youth through sports. *Journal of Adolescent Health, 62*(1), 5–13. https://doi.org/10.1016/j.jadohealth.2017.06.016

Buchanan, L., Kelly, B., Yeatman, H., & Kariippanon, K. (2018). The effects of digital marketing of unhealthy commodities on young people: A systematic review. *Nutrients, 10*(2), 148. https://doi.org/10.3390/nu10020148

Carter, M.-A., Signal, L., Edwards, R., Hoek, J., & Maher, A. (2013). Food, fizzy, and football: Promoting unhealthy food and beverages through sport-a New Zealand case study. *BMC Public Health, 13*(1), 1–7. https://doi.org/10.1186/1471-2458-13-126

Chambers, T., & Sassi, F. (2019). Unhealthy sponsorship of sport. Tougher and more comprehensive regulation is long overdue. *BMJ, 19*, 367:l6718. https://doi.org/10.1136/bmj.l6718

Chambers, T., Signal, L., Carter, M.-A., McConville, S., Wong, R., & Zhu, W. (2017). Alcohol sponsorship of a summer of sport: A frequency analysis of alcohol marketing during major sports events on New Zealand television. *NZMJ, 130*(1448), 27–33. https://www.nzma.org.nz/journal-articles/alcohol-sponsorship-of-a-summer-of-sport-a-frequency-analysis-of-alcohol-marketing-during-major-sports-events-on-new-zealand-television

Cliffe, S. J., & Motion, J. (2005). Building contemporary brands: A sponsorship-based strategy. *Journal of Business Research, 58*(8), 1068–1077. https://doi.org/10.1016/j.jbusres.2004.03.004

Cornwell, T. B. (2020). *Sponsorship in marketing. effective partnerships in sports, arts and events* (Second ed. ed.). Routledge.

Dehghan, S. K. (2019). Coke, crisps, convenience: How ads created a global junk food generation. *The Guardian*, 26 December 2019. [accessed 9 November 2020]., available https://www.theguardian.com/global-development/2019/dec/26/coke-crisps-convenience-how-ads-created-a-global-junk-food-generation?

Dixon, H., Lee, A., & Scully, M. (2019). Sports sponsorship as a cause of obesity. *Current obesity reports, 8*(4), 480–494. https://link.springer.com/article/10.1007/s13679-019-00363-z

Djohari, N., Weston, G., Cassidy, R., Wemyss, M., & Thomas, S. (2019). Recall and awareness of gambling advertising and sponsorship in sport in the UK: A study of young people and adults. *Harm Reduction Journal, 16*(1), 24. https://doi.org/10.1186/s12954-019-0291-9

FIFA (2018) *2018 FIFA world cup Russia, available*: https://resources.fifa.com/image/upload/njqsntrvdvqv8ho1dag5.pdf [accessed 9 November 2020].

Forde, H., White, M., Levy, L., Greaves, F., Hammond, D., Vanderlee, L., Sharp, S., & Adams, J. (2019). The relationship between self-reported exposure to sugar-sweetened beverage promotions and intake: cross-sectional analysis of the 2017 international food policy study. *Nutrients, 11*(12), 3047. https://doi.org/10.3390/nu11123047

Giulianotti, R., & Robertson, R. (2009). *Globalization & Football*. SAGE.

Graham, A., & Adams, J. (2014). Alcohol marketing in televised English professional football: A frequency analysis. *Alcohol and Alcoholism, 49*(3), 343–348. https://doi.org/10.1093/alcalc/agt140

Hall, C. M. (2006). Urban entrepreneurship, corporate interests and sports mega-events: The thin policies of competitiveness within the hard outcomes of neoliberalism. *The Sociological Review, 54*(2Suppl), 59–70. https://doi.org/10.1111/j.1467-954X.2006.00653.x

Harris, J. L., Brownell, K. D., & Bargh, J. A. (2009). The food marketing defense model: Integrating psychological research to protect youth and inform public policy. *Soc Issues Policy Rev*, *3*(1), 211–271. https://doi.org/10.1111/j.1751-2409.2009.01015.x

Harris, J. L., Yokum, S., & Fleming-Milici, F. (2021). Hooked on junk: Emerging evidence on how food marketing affects adolescents' diets and long-term health. *Current Addiction Reports*, *8*(1), 19–27. http://dx.doi.org/10.1007/s40429-020-00346-4 available

Horne, J., & Manzenreiter, W. (2006). An introduction to the sociology of sports mega-events. In J. Horne & W. Manzenreiter (Eds.), *Sports mega-events. social scientific analyses of a global phenomenon*, (pp. 1–24) Blackwell.

Ireland, R., Bunn, C., Chambers, S., Reith, G., & Viggars, M. (2021). How unhealthy commodity industries find a global audience in the English Premier League. three case studies of brand engagement. In *Soccer & society (in publication)*.

Ireland, R., Bunn, C., Reith, G., Philpott, M., Capewell, S., Boyland, E., & Chambers, S. (2019). Commercial determinants of health: Advertising of alcohol and unhealthy foods during sporting events. *Bull World Health Organ*, *97*(4), 290–295. https://doi.org/10.2471/BLT.18.220087

Karg, A., & Lock, D. (2014). Using new media to engage consumers at the football World Cup. In S. Frawley & D. Adair (Eds.), *Managing the football world cup*. Palgrave Macmillan.

Kelly, B., Baur, L. A., Bauman, A. E., King, L., Chapman, K., & Smith, B. J. (2010). Food and drink sponsorship of childrens' sport in Australia: Who pays? *Health Promotion International*, *26*(2), 188–195. https://doi.org/10.1093/heapro/daq061

Kelly, B., Baur, L. A., Bauman, A. E., King, L., Chapman, K., & Smith, B. J. (2011). "Food company sponsors are kind, generous and cool": (Mis)conceptions of junior sports players. *International Journal of Behavioral Nutrition and Physical Activity*, *8*(95), 1–7. https://doi.org/10.1186/1479-5868-8-95

Kelly, B., King, L., Chapman, K., Boyland, E. A. E., . B., & Baur, L. (2015). A hierarchy of unhealthy food promotion effects: Identifying methodological approaches and knowledge gaps. *American Journal of Public Health*, *105*(4), e86–e95. http://dx.doi.org/10.2105/AJPH.2014.302476 available

KPMG (2018) *High stakes: The sponsorship and broadcasting value of the FIFA World Cup*, available: https://www.footballbenchmark.com/the_sponsorship_and_broadcasting_value_of_the_fifa_world_cup [accessed 29 December 2018].

Lindsay, S., Thomas, S., Lewis, S., Westberg, K., Moodie, R., & Jones, S. (2013). Eat, drink and gamble: Marketing messages about 'risky' products in an Australian major sporting series. *BMC Public Health*, *13*(1), 719. https://doi.org/10.1186/1471-2458-13-719

Madden, P. A., & Grube, J. W. (1994). 'The frequency and nature of alcohol and tobacco advertising in televised sports, 1990 through 1992'. *American Journal of Public Health*, *84*(2), 2. https://doi.org/10.2105/AJPH.84.2.297

Madrigal, R., Bee, C., & LaBarge, M. (2005). Using the Olympics and FIFA World Cup to enhance global brand equity: A case study of two companies in the payment services category. In J. Amis & T. B. Cornwell (Eds.), *Global sports sponsorship*, (pp. 179–190) Berg.

Manoli, A. E., & Kenyon, J. A. (2019). Football and marketing. In S. Chadwick, D. Parnell, P. Widdop, & C. Anagnostopoulos (Eds.), *Routledge handbook of football business and management* (pp. 88–100). Routledge.

Mathers, C., & Bonita, R. (2009). Current global health status. In R. Beaglehole & R. Bonita (Eds.), *Global public health. A new era*, (pp. 23–61) Oxford University Press.

Meenagahan, T., & O'Sullivan, P. (2001). Editorial: The passionate embrace - consumer response to sponsorship. *Psychology & Marketing*, *18*(2), 87–94. http://3.0.CO;2-Lhttps://doi.org/10.1002/1520-6793(200102)18:2<87::AID-MAR1000>3.0.CO;2-L

Meenaghan, T. (2001). Understanding sponsorship effects. *Psychology & Marketing*, *18*(2), 95–122. http://3.0.CO;2-Hhttps://doi.org/10.1002/1520-6793(200102)18:2<95::AID-MAR1001>3.0.CO;2-H

Morgan, A., Frawley, S., Fujak, H., & Cobourn, S. (2017). Sponsorship and sport mega-events. In S. Frawley (Ed.), *Managing sport mega-events* (pp. 105–120). Routledge.

Norman, J., Kelly, B., Boyland, E., & McMahon, A.-T. (2016). The impact of marketing and advertising on food behaviours: Evaluating the evidence for a causal relationship. *Curr Nutr Rep*, *5*(3), 139–149. https://doi.org/10.1007/s13668-016-0166-6

Nuss, T., Scully, M., Wakefield, M., & Dixon, H. (2019). Unhealthy sport sponsorship at the 2017 AFL grand final: A case study of its frequency, duration and nature. *Australian and New Zealand Journal of Public Health*, *43*(4), 366–372. https://onlinelibrary.wiley.com/doi/full/10.1111/1753-6405.12920

Ofcom (2017) *Children and parents: Media use and attitudes report*, London, available: https://www.ofcom.org.uk/__data/assets/pdf_file/0020/108182/children-parents-media-use-attitudes-2017.pdf [accessed 12 September 2019].

Organisation, W. H. (2018a) *Evaluating implementation of the WHO set of recommendations on the marketing of foods and non-alcoholic beverages to children. Progress, challenges and guidance for next steps in the WHO European Region.*, Copenhagen, available: http://www.euro.who.int/en/health-topics/disease-prevention/nutrition/publications/2018/evaluating-implementation-of-the-who-set-of-recommendations-on-the-marketing-of-foods-and-non-alcoholic-beverages-to-children.-progress,-challenges-and-guidance-for-next-steps-in-the-who-european-region [accessed 9 November 2020].

Organisation, W. H. (2018b) *Noncommunicable diseases. Fact sheet*, *available*: https://www.who.int/news-room/fact-sheets/detail/noncommunicable-diseases [accessed 30 June 2020].

Pracejus, J. W. (2004). Seven psychological mechanisms through which sponsorship can influence consumers. In L. R. Kahle & C. Riley (Eds.), *Sports marketing and the pyschology of marketing*, (pp. 175–189). Lawrence Erlbaum.

Purves, R. I., Critchlow, N., Stead, M., Adams, J., & Brown, K. (2017). Alcohol marketing during the UEFA EURO 2016 football tournament: A frequency analysis. *International Journal of Environmental Research and Public Health*, *14*(704), 704. http://dx.doi.org/10.3390/ijerph14070704 available

Roche, M. (2006). Mega-events and modernity revisited: Globalization and the case of the Olympics. *The Sociological Review*, *54*(2Suppl), 27–40. https://doi.org/10.1111/j.1467-954X.2006.00651.x

Russell, S. J., Croker, H., & Viner, R. M. (2019). The effect of screen advertising on children's dietary intake: A systematic review and meta-analysis. *Obesity Reviews*, *20*(4), 554–568. https://doi.org/10.1111/obr.12812

Semens, A. (2017). Football sponsorship. In J. Hughson, K. Moore, R. Spaaij, & J. Maguire (Eds.), *Routledge handbook of football studies* (pp. 111–123). Routledge.

Shibuya, K. (2003). WHO Framework Convention on Tobacco Control: Development of an evidence based global public health treaty. *BMJ*, *327*(7407), 154–157. https://doi.org/10.1136/bmj.327.7407.154

Solberg, H. A., & Gratton, C. (2014). Broadcasting the World Cup. In S. Frawley & D. Adair (Eds.), *Managing the football world cup*, (pp. 47–62). Palgrave Macmillan.

Stemler, S., & Tsai, J. (2008). Best practices in estimating interrater reliability. In J. W. Osborne (Ed.), *Best practices in quantitative methods* (pp. 29–49). Sage Publications.

Walsh, A. J., & Giulianotti, R. (2001). This sporting mammon: A normative critique of the commodification of sport. *Journal of the Philosophy of Sport*, *28*(1), 53–77. https://doi.org/10.1080/00948705.2001.9714600

Whannel, G. (2009). Television and the transformation of sport. *American Academy of Political and Social Science*, *625*(1), 205–218. https://doi.org/10.1177/0002716209339144

World Health Organisation (2019) *WHO and FIFA team up for health* [press release], available: https://healthpolicy-watch.news/who-and-fifa-team-up-for-health/ [accessed 22 March 2021].

Strategic marketing through sport for development: managing multi-stakeholder partnerships

Andrew Webb and Krystn Orr

ABSTRACT
Previous literature establishes links between strategic marketing through sport and corporate social responsibility (CSR). While many corporations will leverage sports to reinforce their product and corporate brands, others will use sports as a channel for their CSR efforts aimed at tackling grand societal challenges – global issues that are so complex that multi-stakeholder partnerships are needed to make a difference. As these partnerships involve corporations, non-profits, governments, and other concerned stakeholders, implementing CSR campaigns involving multi-stakeholder partnership remains challenging. Through in-depth interviews with 14 corporate partners of a global movement that enriches the lives of individuals identifying with intellectual disabilities through sport, our study proposes a conceptual model that crystallizes how corporate partners are activated by the multi-stakeholder partner – our proposed sport for development Partnership Management Matrix provides insights about the importance of the frequency and formality of connection between multi-stakeholder partners. Accordingly, a discussion about how the frequency and formality of connections can contribute to producing greater brand value than traditional strategic marketing through sports is provided.

Introduction

In a period of rising public concern about complex social problems like child obesity or inclusion of marginalised individuals, corporations are increasingly expected to address grand challenges (Bailey & Breslin, 2021; George et al., 2016). To the extent that, even during this current global pandemic, a majority of corporations still prioritize building long-term problem-solving partnerships as a strategy for reinforcing their reputation and credibility (C & E, 2020). Such partnerships are frequently developed as part of a corporation's identity defining corporate social responsibility (CSR) component of their strategic marketing efforts (Maon et al., 2021). By partnering with agencies who tackle important social causes, corporations are viewed as a good corporate citizen (Biraghi et al., 2017) which positively shapes a corporation's brand identity (Giulianotti, 2015). Furthermore, in today's connected world, corporate branding efforts frequently need to focus on fostering meaningful relationships with diverse stakeholders (Maon et al., 2021). In fact, some authors assert that, in the digital economy, value is actually co-created through collaborations of different actors that share a common purpose (Koch & Windsperger, 2017; Nachira et al., 2007; Senyo et al., 2019). This blurring of boundaries implies that corporate brands have become 'vehicles of meaning that emerge from social interactions between the company and its environment' (Melewar et al., 2012, p. 601).

Previous research asserts that one way a corporation can positively impact their reputation is to focus their CSR efforts on tackling grand challenges (Carlini et al., 2021; Frynas & Yamahaki, 2016; Hennchen & Schrempf-Stirling, 2020). This has led many corporations to build partnerships with agencies, such as sport for development (SFD) organizations (Bardocz-Bencsik & Doczi, 2019) that apply sport to social justice interventions, or strategic and interventionist development (Giulianotti, 2015). Sport has the potential to contribute to the greater good because of its global reach and ability to move social boundaries (Carlini et al., 2021). Yet, 'to successfully develop socially transformative innovations that achieve more systemic change' (Svensson et al., 2020, p. 666), more insights are needed about how multi-stakeholder partnerships are activated and subsequently managed. This is important as corporations deploy considerable resources to manage the complex networks that shape their corporate brands (Biraghi et al., 2017).

For the purpose of this study, grand challenges are 'critical barrier(s) that if removed, would help solve an important societal problem with a high likelihood of global impact through a widespread implementation' (George et al., 2016). Grand challenges are frequently global in scale and are complex in nature and can usually only be tackled by coordinating the efforts of a broad array of collaborators (George et al., 2016). The ability of the SfD sector to get people involved is one reason it was selected as the general research field for this study (Edwards, 2015; Giulianotti, 2011) as SfD agencies have a track record of leveraging the global appeal of sport to address social issues (Banda & Gultresa, 2015; Maslic, 2019; Thorpe, 2016). The general acceptance that sport produces positive impacts has contributed to transforming the SfD landscape, from involving only a handful of non-profit organisations and NGOS in the early 2000s, to an industry that currently includes hundreds of agencies worldwide (Svensson & Woods, 2017). However, as grand challenges are beyond the expertise of any one single entity, new forms of leadership, management, and coordination are needed to successfully operationalize the resulting multi-stakeholder partnerships.

Founded on stakeholder theory (Mena & Palazzo, 2012; Rasche, 2012), multi-stakeholder partnerships mobilise 'diverse sets of corporate and non-corporate stakeholders together as formally defined coequals in sustained forms of interaction' (Moog et al., 2015, p. 469). Power-sharing and co-ownership distinguishes them from cross-sector social partnerships that are frequently led or driven by corporations (Austin & Seitanidi, 2012; Maak & Pless, 2009; Stadtler & Van Wassenhove, 2016). Accordingly, in a network-based perspective of branding (Biraghi et al., 2017), this study provides insights about the activation and management of partners in sport for the development of multi-stakeholder initiatives.

To this end, we will begin by contextualizing CSR, grand challenges, multi-stakeholder partnerships, as well as sport for development. Our review will also serve to introduce Special Olympics Canada (SOC), which was selected as our specific object of research. The subsequent section will explain the methodology used to explore the question of how corporations are activated into collaborating with SfD agencies, and what are the success factors of sustainable multi-stakeholder partnerships. A discussion will synthesize our findings by proposing a conceptual model that we have labelled as the Partnership Management Matrix. Finally, we will conclude by providing implications and limits of our conceptual model.

Literature review

Previous research has highlighted the need for better understanding roles and partnership structures in the context of sport for development (AlKhalifa & Collison, 2020). This is important as many SfD agencies are designed to address grand challenges such as the poverty, inclusion, access to education, and enriching the lives of children facing systemic barriers. One element that makes grand challenges difficult to manage is that they often demand a spectrum of interventions. On the one hand, social issues frequently require local partnerships to deal with community-level elements of a given issue. On the other hand, local actors will likely need to work with global initiatives that bring together dozens, or even hundreds of collaborators to tackle the root causes of global problems. This has been highlighted in the previous research that has demonstrated that many SfD agencies require the help of transnational partnerships to obtain the capacity, sustainability, and expertise necessary to tackle the complex issues they are dealing with (Collison et al., 2016). The resulting networks can be quite extensive. For example, previous research demonstrated that the now defunct United Nations Office on Sport for Development and Peace's network included universities, civil society, individuals, SfD agencies, private sector corporations, governments, social media, and other UN agencies (Richelieu & Webb, 2018). The closing of this office in 2015 shocked the SfD field and led some academics to call for 'more critical discussions on how actors within this field can better connect to channel their expertise toward increased social transformation' (Svensson & Hambrick, 2019). Thus, better understanding how actors in this field connect is vital as the grand challenges they are dealing with 'require coordinated and sustained effort from multiple and diverse stakeholders toward a clearly articulated problem or goal' (George et al., 2016). Accordingly, previous literature has highlighted not only the need for better understanding the conditions in which cross-sector cooperation operations are developed and formalized (Ekholm & Holmlid, 2020) but also 'the need for new and evidence-based solutions for mobilizing stakeholders and resources in sport for development and peace' (Svensson & Loat, 2019, p. 426). Granted, previous research has identified that successful partnerships require more horizontal decision-making than top-down management styles (MacIntosh et al., 2016). However, besides a handful of studies such as Peachey et al. (2018) that have focused on partnership and network development, little research has been conducted on how SfD agencies find, activate, and retain corporate partners who will understand the shifting roles and responsibilities associated with multi-stakeholder partnerships. This study will address this gap.

The complexity of sport for development

The corporate partners included in this study work with a Canadian non-profit agency that uses sport to enrich the lives of athletes identifying with an intellectual disability. In a sense, the partners we studied are like the thousands of businesses that channel significant portions of their strategic marketing efforts through sport. However, the commonplace nature of companies sponsoring sports ironically makes studying such relationships difficult because everyone thinks they understand sports (Bourdieu et al., 1998). As a case in point, there is a stereotype that sport is beneficial (Darnell & Black, 2011) to the extent where many managers would not think twice about supporting a non-profit sports organization. This is reinforced by the fact that sport occupies an important social space in most societies (Frey & Eitzen, 1991). When this taken for granted acceptance of sport is coupled with passionate claims that sport has the power to break down social barriers (Darnell, 2007), the seductive appeal of SfD is understandable.

Yet, it is critical to underscore that despite the potential benefits of sport, there are also a great number of social problems generated by, or associated with, sport (Kidd & Donnelly, 2007). Many SfD agencies leverage purported benefits of sport that go beyond what is gained through sport participation (Haudenhuyse et al., 2013). For instance, previous literature has demonstrated that sport is a social activity that is rife with sexism (Frey & Eitzen, 1991), homophobia (Hayhurst et al., 2014; Schulenkorf, 2017), and racism (Hayhurst, 2016; Sugden, 2010), amongst other critical social issues. Furthermore, overly optimistic claims about the potential of SfD have been described as 'almost evangelical policy rhetoric' (Coalter, 2013) that can lead to incestuous amplification of the supposed, and sometimes mythical (Frey & Eitzen, 1991) potential of SfD programs. Precisely, sport is a global construct that can be beneficial or harmful, depending on how it is operationalized.

However, there are many agencies who are cognizant of sports' cultural baggage (Darnell & Hayhurst, 2011) and have adapted their operations accordingly. Let us now introduce one such agency that was selected as the object of research for this project.

Contextualizing Special Olympics Canada

For centuries, social exclusion, institutionalization (Wilson et al., 2017), and even sterilization (Grekul, 2011) of individuals with intellectual disabilities were common practices. These practices were based on the dominant thought of the day that assumed that an intellectual disability somehow prevented someone from understanding the principles of society, including sport. However, in the late 1960s, Dr. Frank Hayden demonstrated that it was not the intellectual disability that prevents someone from practicing sport, rather the primary barrier was simply the lack of opportunity to practice sports (Webb et al., 2019). The movement Dr. Hayden founded with Eunice Shriver in 1968 has become a global force for change. Currently operating in 172 countries and serving over 5 million athletes worldwide, Special Olympics (SO) is the world's largest sports organization dedicated to enriching lives through sports of individuals living with intellectual disability (Shriver, 2015). Moreover, the longevity of this organisation and its reach are two factors that distinguishes SO with many other SfD NGOs who still struggle to gain legitimacy in the eyes of their partners (Hayhurst & Frisby, 2010).

For the purposes of designing a manageable study, we focused on Special Olympics Canada (www.specialolympics.ca), which is one of the oldest chapters in the world (Harada et al., 2011). SOC currently operates a federated model that accredits 12 provincial and territorial chapters. With the help of 22 major sponsors and over 20,000 volunteers, this multi-stakeholder partnership offers 18 summer and winter sports to over

49,000 athletes. Through events such as local, national, and world games, as well as ancillary events such as galas and awareness events, SOC is a driver of social change and inclusion for all (Harada et al., 2011). An example of their reach is the Global Day of Inclusion. Started in 2018, this event produced, in Canada alone, 91.1 million media posts and generated some 211.6 million impressions on social media (https://www.specialolympics.ca/about/financials-impact-reports). When considering that it took only about 50 years for this force for change to help tear down exclusionary attitudes and misguided practices that were constructed over several millennia, not only is their impact remarkable, but their sustainability is as well. This is all the more impressive when previous research has identified sustainability as a major issue for most SfD agencies (Whitley & Welty Peachey, 2020). Yet, as the grand challenge of inclusion is competing with hundreds of other important social issues, the question of how corporations are activated into supporting this cause over others remains. Let us now present our methodology and research questions.

Methods and methodology

Research objectives and questions

The overall purpose of this study was to understand sponsors' experience and perspectives of the practical components that foster or hinder engaging in a corporate partnership with SOC. Two overarching research questions guided this study:

(1) How are corporations activated to engage with SfD?
(2) Why do corporations remain involved with SfD organizations such as SOC?

Design

Inductive methods were selected as they excel in situations for 'which there is limited theory and on problems without clear answer' (Eisenhardt et al., 2016, p. 1113). As we focus on the dynamics of one setting (Eisenhardt, 1989), we adopted an interpretive perspective to explore the subjective reality of the partnership (Williams, 2000). While SOC partnerships remained our main object of research, all sponsors were considered as concomitant cases and we approached each partner with the intention of becoming 'intimately familiar with each case as a stand-alone entity' (Eisenhardt, 1989, p. 540). This design facilitated the understanding of cross-case patterns.

Recruitment and data collection

To achieve this project's goals, it was essential to gain the perspectives of SOC partners on the practical and managerial components of their partnership. Accordingly, senior managers, directors, and CEOs of all 22 SOC corporate partners were invited to participate by the CEO of SOC. As a point of clarity, the term 'partner' is retained for this paper as it is the typology SOC uses to describe its corporate partners. SOC's CEO had no knowledge of who consented to participate nor had access to any raw data. Out of this potential sample of 22 partners, 4 women and 10 men agreed to participate and will be identified with generic numbers to ensure confidentiality. Moreover, as SOC recognizes different levels of corporate sponsors, our research is representative of the available data set as we have included representatives from four of the six categories of SOC sponsorships ranging from *Bronze and Friends* to *Diamond*. Interviews, lasting between 50 and 90 minutes, were audio recorded, transcribed, and coded using reflexive thematic analysis (V. Braun & Clarke, 2006; Braun et al., 2016; Virginia Braun & Clarke, 2019) as well as interpretive phenomenological analysis (IPA).

Analysis

The first author conducted a deductive thematic analysis, following Braun et al.'s (2016) six phases: familiarization, coding, theme development, theme refinement, theme naming, and writing of the manuscript. The first author used an Actor-Network Theory (ANT) lens to provide insights on how both humans and non-humans interact to produce effects (Callon, 1986; Latour, 2005). In ANT, power, influence, or the ability to tackle a grand challenge are produced by the ongoing connection and activation of a network of actors, who attempt to change, or translate, the current state of affairs, into a new state. As context is always evolving, ensuring the cohesion and mobilization of actors is a task that requires constant attention from the human managers of the network. Moreover, extensive role negotiations occur and stabilize within the network. Without role stabilization, reduction in controversies and alignment of interests, the network would likely not produce effects (Latour, 2005). Thus, while interview transcriptions formed our primary data, the researchers took field notes on what was observed of the corporate offices during in-person interviews ($n = 7$), as well as on the content of corporate websites, and publicly accessible documents (e.g., annual reports). Specifically, we were looking for SOC material (e.g., posters, logo, photos, artefacts) displayed in public spaces or offices. These observations informed us about the sponsor's relationship with SOC.

Aligning with Eisenhardt's (1989) recommendation to obtain multiple perspectives, an IPA approach was also adopted as this method has been applied in the previous SfD research (D'Angelo et al., 2020). IPA explores a specific object or event (a case) that is unique to the individual while recognizing the dynamic process and active role of the researcher(s) throughout (Smith & Shinebourne, 2012). Thus, the participants are simultaneously making sense of their lived experience, while the researchers are making sense of the participants' understandings of their world, otherwise known as a double hermeneutic (e.g., Armitage et al., 2020). As such, the researchers attempted to understand the participants' perspectives on their partnerships with SOC while being critical of what is being said and the interpretations being made. Additionally, IPA privileges the lived experience (e.g., sponsors' experiences of the partnership), hermeneutics (e.g., interview and focus within the discussions), interpretive layers (e.g., combined descriptive overview with theoretical lenses and the development of a new model), and what has been called the 'gem' – a quote that stands out (e.g., each quadrant of the new model is exemplified by a direct quote from a sponsor) (Eatough & Smith, 2017).

Rigor

Institutional ethical approval was granted prior to commencement of this project, and in an attempt to be as rigorous as possible (e.g., Maine et al., 2020), the authors have been transparent in their perspectives and processes throughout the research process. We have situated our participants in their demographics and roles with their corporations in partnership with SOC, provided sample quotes throughout the 'Findings' section, described the collated perspectives as coherently as possible with critical interpretations as necessary to answer our research questions, and considered each of these components with respect to the reader. Additionally, to challenge the critical interpretations and credibility of the results that the first author put forth, the second author acted as a critical friend (Stolle et al., 2018).

Moreover, the authors wish to disclose that we identify as a White man and woman with the privilege of higher education in exercise and sport psychology, and management. We do not identify with a disability. Both authors have partnered with SOC and Special Olympics Ontario over the last 5 years.

Findings and discussion

By concurrently considering a) the lived experiences of corporate partners currently operating in a multi-stakeholder partnership designed take on the grand challenge of enriching lives of individuals living with an intellectual disability, with b) theoretical perspectives on CSR-driven strategic marketing efforts that reinforce or (re)present corporate brands through partnerships with sports agencies, three main themes emerge. First, *Unique Decision Pathways* describes how each partner distinctly came to their partnership with SOC. This will lead to a second theme in which we conceptualize a Partnership Management Matrix that synthesizes how SOC activates, then manages their partnerships. The third theme examines the effects of the successful implementation of the Partnership Management Matrix as we introduce and discuss the concept of *partnership equity* that crystallizes the value partners perceive they gain through their involvement with SOC over time.

First theme – unique decision pathways

The first theme explores the many decision-making processes managers take to get involved in such a partnership as theirs with SOC. For instance, some partners participated in, or led, the decision-making process, whereas others inherited the relationship when taking on their position. For example, Partner #4 explained that the action of getting involved began with a strategic marketing decision made by their corporate headquarters to globally donate $1 billion US dollars over 10 years to grand challenges. Yet, each national office selected the social cause they wanted to adopt. This led to a localized approach to selecting their partnership, in which they strategically decided that real impact could only be produced through a long-term partnership. The pathway they adopted involved 'light touch discussions' with several non-profits located in their region, identifying those with *bold mission*, then selecting one organisation that had a stable management team with whom they 'clicked.'

Other partners also took structured approaches to selecting which agencies to support. Working for national firms, Partners #5, 7, and 13 put calls out to their provincial representatives to see which social causes they were working with, and Special Olympics frequently came up. In what may be described as a structured, yet decentralised decision-making pathway, regional managers influenced corporate strategic marketing decisions. They did this because they loved doing stewardship work with SOC athletes as 'they're down to earth and funny. They appreciate everything, like anything, and sure they want to win medals, but they are more worried about their friends. There is enormous value in their perspectives' (Partner #5). Thus, for this firm, it was the breadth (i.e., national reach) and depth (i.e., a presence in many towns and boroughs) that was a key factor for implementing a nationwide strategic marketing campaign with SOC.

Other partners (i.e., Partners # 6) made the decision alone, but in a deliberate and planned process. Still, others (i.e., Partners #2,3) took informal approaches based on personal contacts that connected them to SOC. Overall, such partnerships began simply with an 'ask' from SOC. For instance, one of their contacts would ask for help with a specific element of the SOC's annual fundraising gala or with an upcoming sporting event. The initial contact would lead to other interactions and the partnership would flow from there. As such, fundraising events have previously been identified as being instrumental in contributing to a SFD organization's financial capacity (Clutterbuck & Doherty, 2019; Svensson & Hambrick, 2016; Svensson et al., 2017) and long-term success. Yet, the potential for fundraising events to indirectly contribute to partnership development has perhaps been neglected. In fact, for several partners, events and Games played a significant role in their activation pathways, such as Partner #6 who mentioned being converted 'like an evangelist' for the SOC movement after attending the National Summer Games in Vancouver. At these events, guests hear the athletes speak and can see the impact SOC has on the athletes' lives. Such experiences often lend to exclamations such as, 'wow, this is an incredible organization! What are they doing for next year? What can I help with?' (Partner #6). Thus, the decision-making pathway theme suggests that partners have nuanced activation routes that include making either a structured or informal decision, as well as making the decision to get involved either alone in a team. Let us now examine how SOC influences their partners' decision-making.

Second theme – the partnership management matrix

In this section, we shift our perspective somewhat and draw out what factors influence this pathway. Accordingly, in this section, we will propose a conceptual model that crystallizes two factors that first activate and then contribute to the maintenance of the partnerships that produce the effects and impacts of CSR-driven strategic marketing through sport for development.

Our data suggests that awareness, interest, mobilization, and enrollment in a cause are still frequently produced by a variety of traditional means, such as written, visual, and electronic assets. But our analysis also suggests that activation is a nuanced concept. For many partners, activation occurs after direct contact with athletes. Time and again, partners relate that watching athletes compete, hearing them speak during a gala, or even chatting with them at a BBQ, is what made them 'click' with this cause. The authenticity, the unexpected sporting ability, or sometimes simply speaking with someone with an intellectual disability for the first time in their life, was what ultimately activated many partners.

Yet, one important finding is that partnership pathways are very different for each partner. This suggests that different types of partners need different types of connections. For instance, some partners reported needing formalized connections such as those provided by audited annual reports, reach reports, or invitations to the VIP section of the annual Limitless Gala and/or to the World Games. Alternatively, other partners were content with a phone call, a small but significant gift that they can expose in their office, or with an occasional post-card from a sponsored athlete. This idea is conceptualized as *the formality of connections*.

Another recurring theme was the *frequency of connections* which conceptualises the desire of some partners for frequent and predetermined contact, whilst others were comfortable with the occasional or impromptu phone call or ask for help. By collating the partners according to their expressed need for specific connection formality and frequency, four partner archetypes inductively emerged from our analysis: advocates, adjuvants, allies, and ambassadors. Combining the connection formality and frequency with the partner typology produces what we label as a strategic Partnership Management Matrix as presented in Figure 1. Overall, this matrix provides new perspectives on how an agency dedicated to taking on a grand challenge can tailor its connections to fit the needs of different types of partners in their multi-stakeholder partnership.

Put differently, activation and maintenance of multi-stakeholder partnerships may be achieved by adjusting the *frequency* and *formality of connections* according to the partner's needs. Considering the four partner archetypes presented in Figure 1 offers valuable implications for partnership building efforts. One implication is that an agency could now operationalise the frequency and formality of connections based on the type of strategic partner they are looking for – targeting adjuvants will be done differently than ambassadors. Importantly, getting the fit right can have considerable impacts as several of the partners in this project have been a stakeholder in SOC for 25–30 years strong. Thus, over time, becoming part of the SOC movement can even lead to corporations assuming co-ownership (Yin & Jamali, 2020) of social causes, such as enriching lives of individuals living with intellectual disabilities. Granted, trust, and a scandal-free history of SOC were mentioned by partners as important retention

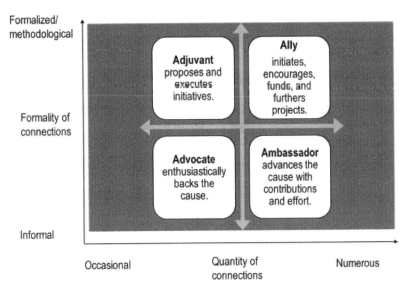

Figure 1. The Partnership Management Matrix.

factors. Yet, we assert that the appropriate frequency and formality of connections are critical for encouraging partners to 'stick around' long enough to develop a sense of ownership of the multi-stakeholder partnerships. Over time, this produces what we label as partnership equity.

Third theme – partnership equity

As multi-stakeholder co-creation of brands (Zhang et al., 2015) has replaced traditional product branding, understanding the building blocks of sustainable multi-stakeholder partnerships is essential for successfully operationalizing strategic marketing efforts through sport. Understanding how corporate brands are built through authentic partnerships is perhaps more important now than ever. Indeed, the rise in the digital economy has led certain scholars to suggest that brand image and reputation is now primarily generated through the partnerships brands develop (Foroudi et al., 2020) and that brand value is co-created through open and flexible collaboration (Koch & Windsperger, 2017; Nachira et al., 2007; Senyo et al., 2019).

When we collate the partners' narratives, the third recurring theme that emerged was that getting the connection frequency and formality right produces value for the partners. One such value could be described as *partnership equity* that provides, over time, both individual and brand value.

Partnership Equity and Brand Value

As many partners have been with SOC for over 25 years (i.e., Partners #, 5, 6, 7,8,10) the longstanding nature of their relationship produces partnership equity. For example, Partner #8 explained that because of the acquired partnership equity, stopping, or even altering the relationship becomes more difficult over time – working with SOC has become second nature as in something they now do naturally. Such accumulated partnership equity has tangible effects on the firm. For example, Partner #10 explained that many of their regional outlets have become, over time, increasingly inclined to hire SOC athletes. The partnership equity here was manifested in a shift in HR practices that actually increased employee morale. Specifically, the 'miscalculated and unexpected authenticity of people with intellectual disabilities' (Partner #10) had a significant positive impact on this firm's team spirit. This same partner explained that beyond the operational benefits to their outlets, their overarching strategic marketing goal with this partnership was directly related to their corporate brand. In short, their aim is to be the number one brand, or in their words 'top of mind brand,' associated with SOC. They explained that they currently use a celebrity sports star as a brand ambassador and that they have research that demonstrates that when consumers think of this athlete, they think of their brand – they want to have that same top of mind effect when people think of SOC.

Partnership Equity and Individual Value

For others, partnership equity was less about the direct impact on the brand and more about personal value. As explained by Partner #8, there is a general sentiment that, *there's something pure about Special Olympics. I think for a lot of us, it's not about the money, it's not about the contacts, it's not about the signage – it's about the pure joy of running, jumping, swimming, throwing, whatever it is they're doing. It's just joyful.*

Partnership equity was also produced individual value during games and events. For example, partner #3 explained that:

I was put in a soccer competition with a Special Olympics athlete, and had my ass kicked there. Then there were three of us that went up against a golfer. She dropped hers within two feet of the hole. We were like eight feet some of us. And it was all done on Face Time Live and then posted. I loved it; I had a fantastic time.

Thus, informal ancillary events are arguably not only valuable for attracting the attention of potential partners but also for strategically retaining individual partners who decide which grand challenges to take on. Partner #8 also explained that the individual value their managers gain is one of the key reasons why they have been a partner for over 30 years. Other partners, such as Partner #6, explained that the steady growth in partnership equity they obtain through an association with SOC produced what they called 'organisational stickiness' which is the metaphor they use to explain why they have been helping SOC out for 25 years. Moreover, another reason for this stickiness was that Partner #6's staff loved the authenticity of helping to make the world a better place as this provides a refreshing break from what they called the 'regular consumerism of pushing various products'. Similarly, Partner #3 explained that they are not helping SOC with the intent to make their business grow, rather that they were seeking partnership equity that was really about the:

Pleasure of seeing how these individuals compete and their appreciation they have for a chance to compete, and the chance to be with the athletes. And when there are events, a lot of our people put their hand up to go help out. I mean office people put their hands up to go help out in the installation. People enjoy helping out.

The importance of providing opportunities for staff to work directly on SOC projects was also highlighted as a valued activity by Partner #4:

We're in the talent business. So, attracting, retaining the very best talent is what allows us to win and succeed and grow the way we have. And, you know, consistently we hear that actually being able to make contributions to not-for-profit causes is a very important attribute for people when they think about joining and staying with a company like ours.

Thus, while partners are unanimously happy to help out, there are also clear business advantages reported by partners that have decided to underpin their strategic marketing through SfD.

Finally, and possibly most importantly, getting the formality and frequency of connections right for each of the four partner archetypes has the potential to produce an amazing, and admittedly unexpected, effect: Several partners spoke of love:

"I do this because I **love** to do this." (Partner #3)

"They are really happy to see us, we're happy to see them, our team **loves** to work with them." (Partner #4)

"When you know you really are doing something good is sometimes few and far between . . . . I always **loved** to have these opportunities. I felt great about them." (Partner #6)

*"These are the events I **love** the most because I went out with a colleague, we did it as a group and it was so fun and the energy was great and our New CEO **loved** the SOC partnership and connected right away." (Partner #7)*

*"I just **love** them. I **love** the athletes, and I **love** that they could graciously challenge us more." (Partner #8)*

*"We do it because we **love** it." (Partner #9)*

Undoubtedly love is a powerful, yet elusive effect, to the point where this love should perhaps be the ultimate goal of strategic marketing through sport. Thus, achieving the perfect fit between the frequency and formality of connections arguably has the potential to contribute to not only brand value but also to building the collaborations, trust, and love needed to take on grand challenges.

Implications, limits, and avenues for future research

As in all research, this paper has limits that need to be recognized. First, our data set consists only of current partners. More research is needed to examine corporations that decided to stop their relationship with SOC, or to not get involved in the first place. This suggests that more research is needed to better understand if our Partnership Management Matrix would provide insights into other not-for-profit sports. This effort could examine local sports clubs as well as large international agencies, such as the FC Barcelona foundation, the International Olympics Committee, the International Paralympic Committee, or the National Collegiate Athletic Association. Other limits may be drawn from the partner's narratives themselves. For instance, Partner #8 mentioned that the personal connection to the athletes was key, but that these connections were often limited to the higher-level managers. Investigating how staff understand partnerships would also be valuable. This also suggests that more research is needed on both macro, such as power dynamics, and micro issues related to the management of coalitions and partnerships.

Yet, even with these limits, this paper offers timely implications. For the corporate manager who is considering implementing strategic marketing through sport, our matrix may provide a way to select a cause that offers the frequency and formality of connections they require. For sports management and marketing scholars, our matrix may provide valuable perspectives on building theory about resilient and impactful partnerships.

Conclusion

In this paper, we propose a typology that categorises partners according to the frequency and formality of connections they require from a multi-stakeholder partnership. The resulting Advocate, Adjuvant, Ambassadors, and Ally typologies can help multi-stakeholder partnerships to adjust their connection efforts, allow corporations to increase the effectiveness and efficiency of their strategic marketing efforts, and provide scholars with new perspectives for understanding multi-stakeholder partnerships in action. By understanding that each partner requires a different frequency and formality of connection, the courageous collectives that decide to take on grand challenges will conceivably be better equipped to make a positive impact on society.

Acknowledgments

The author wishes to acknowledge the support given by Special Olympics Canada. We also acknowledge that this research took place on the traditional territory of the Mississaugas of the Credit, the Anishnabeg, the Chippewa, the Haudenosaunee, and the Wendat peoples and is now home to many diverse First Nations, Inuit, and Métis peoples. We also acknowledge this land is covered by Treaty 13 signed with the Mississaugas of the Credit and the Williams Treaties signed with multiple Mississaugas and Chippewa bands.

Disclosure statement

The author declares that there is no conflict of interest associated with this research.

Funding

Funding for this research was obtained through the author's research fund provided by Carleton University as well as through the Stands for Social Sciences and Humanities Research Council (SSHRC) Partnership engage fund

ORCID

Andrew Webb http://orcid.org/0000-0001-8042-963X
Krystn Orr http://orcid.org/0000-0002-9938-9655

References

AlKhalifa, H. K., & Collison, H. (2020). Adapting to local context and managing relationships: A case study of a multinational SDP partnership in Bahrain. *Journal of Global Sport Management*, 1–21. https://doi.org/10.1080/24704067.2020.1805162

Armitage, S., Parkinson, M., Halligan, S., & Reynolds, S. (2020). Mothers' experiences of having an adolescent child with depression: An interpretative phenomenological analysis. *Journal of Child and Family Studies*, 29(6), 1617–1629. https://doi.org/10.1007/s10826-020-01705-5

Austin, J. E., & Seitanidi, M. M. (2012). Collaborative value creation: A review of partnering between nonprofits and businesses: Part I. Value creation spectrum and collaboration stages. *Nonprofit and Voluntary Sector Quarterly*, 41(5), 726–758. https://doi.org/10.1177/0899764012450777

Bailey, K., & Breslin, D. (2021). The COVID-19 pandemic: What can we learn from past research in organizations and management? *International Journal of Management Reviews*, 23(1), 3–6. https://doi.org/10.1111/ijmr.12237

Banda, D., & Gultresa, I. (2015). Using global south sport-for-development experiences to inform global north CSR design and implementation: A case study of Euroleague basketball's one team programme. *Corporate Governance*, 15(2), 196–213. https://doi.org/10.1108/CG-08-2014-0100

Bardocz-Bencsik, M., & Doczi, T. (2019). Mapping sport for development and peace as bourdieu's field. *Physical Culture and Sport, Studies and Research*, 81(1), 1–12. https://doi.org/10.2478/pcssr-2019-0001

Biraghi, S., Gambetti, R. C., & Schultz, D. E. (2017). Advancing a citizenship approach to corporate branding: A societal view. *International Studies of Management and Organization*, *47*(2), 206–215. https://doi.org/10.1080/00208825.2017.1256168

Bourdieu, P., Dauncey, H., & Hare, G. (1998). The state, economics and sport. *Culture, Sport, Society*, *1*(2), 15–21. https://doi.org/10.1080/14610989808721813

Braun, V., & Clarke, V. (2006). Using thematic analysis in psychology. *Qualitative Research in Psychology*, *3*(2), 77–101. https://doi.org/10.1191/1478088706qp063oa

Braun, V., & Clarke, V. (2019). Reflecting on reflexive thematic analysis. *Qualitative Research in Sport, Exercise and Health*, *11*(4), 589–597. https://doi.org/10.1080/2159676X.2019.1628806

Braun, V., Clarke, V., & Weate, P. (2016). Using thematic analysis in sport and exercise research. In B. Smith & A. C. Spakes (Eds.), *Routledge Handbook of Qualitative Research in Sport and Exercise* (pp. 191–205). Routledge

C & E. (2020). *C & E corporate-NGO partnerships barometer headline findings resilience amidst the turbulence*. https://www.candeadvisory.com/sites/candeadvisory.com/files/C%26E-Corporate-NGO-Partnerships-Barometer-20-Headline-findings.pdf

Callon, M. (1986). Some elements of a sociology of translation: Domestication of the scallops and the fishermen of Saint-Brieuc Bay. In J. Law (Ed.), *Power, action and belief: A new sociology of knowledge?* (pp. 196–223). Routledge. https://doi.org/10.22394/0869-5377-2017-2-49-90

Carlini, J., Pavlidis, A., Thomson, A., & Morrison, C. (2021). Delivering on social good - corporate social responsibility and professional sport: A systematic quantitative literature review. *Journal of Strategic Marketing*, 1–14. https://doi.org/10.1080/0965254X.2021.1881147

Clutterbuck, R., & Doherty, A. (2019). Organizational capacity for domestic sport for development. *Journal of Sport for Development*, *7*(12), 16–32.

Coalter, F. (2013). *Sport for development: What game are we playing?* Routledge.

Collison, H., Darnell, S., Giulianotti, R., & Howe, P. D. (2016). Sport for social change and development: sustaining transnational partnerships and adapting international curriculums to local contexts in rwanda. *International Journal of the History of Sport*, *33*(15), 1685–1699. https://doi.org/10.1080/09523367.2017.1318850

D'Angelo, C., Corvino, C., Cianci, E., & Gozzoli, C. (2020). Sport for vulnerable youth: The role of multi-professional groups in sustaining intersectoral collaboration. *Social Inclusion*, *8*(3), 129–138. https://doi.org/10.17645/si.v8i3.2745

Darnell. (2007). Playing with race: Right to Play and the production of whiteness in "development through sport. *Sport in Society: Cultures, Commerce, Media, Politics*, *10*(4), 19. https://doi.org/10.1080/17430430701388756

Darnell, & Black, D. (2011). Mainstreaming sport into international development studies. *Third World Quarterly*, *32*(3), 367–378. https://doi.org/10.1080/01436597.2011.573934

Darnell, S., & Hayhurst, L. M. C. (2011). Sport for decolonization: Exploring a new praxis of sport for development. *Progress in Development Studies*, *11*(3), 183–196. https://doi.org/10.1177/146499341001100301

Donnelly, P., & Kidd, B. (2007). Literature Reviews on Sport for Development. In *Sport for Development & Peace. International Working Group*. University of Toronto, Faculty of Physical Education and Health.(pp. 1–195)

Eatough, V., & Smith, J. (2017). *BIROn - Birkbeck Institutional research online interpretative phenomenological analysis*.

Edwards, M. B. (2015). The role of sport in community capacity building: An examination of sport for development research and practice. *Sport Management Review*, *18*(1), 6–19. https://doi.org/10.1016/j.smr.2013.08.008

Eisenhardt, K. M. (1989). Building theories from case study research. *Academy of Management Review*, *14*(4), 532–550. https://doi.org/10.5465/amr.1989.4308385

Eisenhardt, K. M., Graebner, M. E., & Sonenshein, S. (2016). Grand challenges and inductive methods: Rigor without rigor mortis. *Academy of Management Journal*, *59*(4), 1113–1123. https://doi.org/10.5465/amj.2016.4004

Ekholm, D., & Holmlid, S. (2020). Formalizing sports-based interventions in cross-sectoral cooperation : Governing and infrastructuring practice, program, and preconditions. *Journal of Sport for Development*, 8(14), 1–20.

Foroudi, P., Nazarian, A., Ziyadin, S., Kitchen, P., Hafeez, K., Priporas, C., & Pantano, E. (2020). Co-creating brand image and reputation through stakeholder's social network. *Journal of Business Research*, 114(March), 42–59. https://doi.org/10.1016/j.jbusres.2020.03.035

Frey, J. H., & Eitzen, D. S. (1991). Sport and society. *Annual Review of Sociology*, 17(1), 503–522. https://doi.org/10.1146/annurev.so.17.080191.002443

Frynas, J. G., & Yamahaki, C. (2016). Corporate social responsibility: Review and roadmap of theoretical perspectives. *Business Ethics*, 25(3), 258–285. https://doi.org/10.1111/beer.12115

George, G., Howard-Grenville, J., Joshi, A., & Tihanyi, L. (2016). Understanding and tackling societal grand challenges through management research. *Academy of Management Journal*, 59(6), 1880–1895. https://doi.org/10.5465/amj.2016.4007

Giulianotti, R. (2011). Sport, transnational peacemaking, and global civil society: Exploring the reflective discourses of "sport, development, and peace" project officials. *Journal of Sport and Social Issues*, 35(1), 50–71. https://doi.org/10.1177/0193723510396666

Giulianotti, R. (2015). Corporate social responsibility in sport: Critical issues and future possibilities. *Corporate Governance*, 15(2), 243–248. https://doi.org/10.1108/CG-10-2014-0120

Grekul, J. (2011). A well-oiled machine: Alberta's Eugenics program, 1928-1972. *Alberta History*, 59(3), 16–24.

Harada, C. M., Siperstein, G. N., Parker, R. C., & Lenox, D. (2011). Promoting social inclusion for people with intellectual disabilities through sport: Special olympics international, global sport initiatives and strategies. *Sport in Society*, 14(9), 1131–1148. https://doi.org/10.1080/17430437.2011.614770

Haudenhuyse, R., Theeboom, M., & Nols, Z. (2013). Sports-based interventions for socially vulnerable youth: Towards well-defined interventions with easy-to-follow outcomes? *International Review for the Sociology of Sport*, 48(4), 471–484. https://doi.org/10.1177/1012690212448002

Hayhurst, & Frisby, W. (2010). Inevitable tensions: Swiss and Canadian sport for development NGO perspectives on partnerships with high performance sport. *European Sport Management Quarterly*, 10(1), 75–96. https://doi.org/10.1080/16184740903554140

Hayhurst, L. M. C. (2016). Sport for development and peace: A call for transnational, multi-sited, postcolonial feminist research. *Qualitative Research in Sport, Exercise and Health*, 8(5), 424–443. https://doi.org/10.1080/2159676X.2015.1056824

Hayhurst, L. M. C., MacNeill, M., Kidd, B., & Knoppers, A. (2014). Gender relations, gender-based violence and sport for development and peace: Questions, concerns and cautions emerging from Uganda. *Women's Studies International Forum*, 47(PA), 157–167. https://doi.org/10.1016/j.wsif.2014.07.011

Hennchen, E., & Schrempf-Stirling, J. (2020). Fit for addressing grand challenges? A process model for effective accountability relationships within multi-stakeholder initiatives in developing countries. *Business Ethics*, 2018, 1–20. https://doi.org/10.1111/beer.12325

Koch, T., & Windsperger, J. (2017). Seeing through the network: Competitive advantage in the digital economy. *Journal of Organization Design*, 6(1). https://doi.org/10.1186/s41469-017-0016-z

Latour, B. (2005). *Reassembling the social: An introduction to actor-network-theory*. Oxford University Press.

Maak, T., & Pless, N. M. (2009). Business leaders as citizens of the world. Advancing humanism on a global scale. *Journal of Business Ethics*, 88(3), 537–550. https://doi.org/10.1007/s10551-009-0122-0

MacIntosh, E., Arellano, A., & Forneris, T. (2016). Exploring the community and external-agency partnership in sport-for-development programming. *European Sport Management Quarterly*, 16(1), 38–57. https://doi.org/10.1080/16184742.2015.1092564

Maine, A., Brown, M., Dickson, A., & Truesdale, M. (2020). The experience of type 2 diabetes self-management in adults with intellectual disabilities and their caregivers: A review of the literature using meta-aggregative synthesis and an appraisal of rigor. *Journal of Intellectual Disabilities*, 24(2), 253–267. https://doi.org/10.1177/1744629518774172

Maon, F., Swaen, V., & De Roeck, K. (2021). Corporate branding and corporate social responsibility: Toward a multi-stakeholder interpretive perspective. *Journal of Business Research*, 126 (October2019), 64–77. https://doi.org/10.1016/j.jbusres.2020.12.057

Maslic, V. (2019). *CrossFit sarajevo : Positioning against dominant ethnonational narratives* 7 3–4.

Melewar, T. C., Gotsi, M., & Andriopoulos, C. (2012). Shaping the research agenda for corporate branding: Avenues for future research. *European Journal of Marketing*, 46(5), 600–608. https://doi.org/10.1108/03090561211235138

Mena, S., & Palazzo, G. (2012). Input and output legitimacy of multi-stakeholder initiatives. *Business Ethics Quarterly*, 22(3), 527–556. https://doi.org/10.5840/beq201222333

Moog, S., Spicer, A., & Böhm, S. (2015). The politics of multi-stakeholder initiatives: The crisis of the forest stewardship council. *Journal of Business Ethics*, 128(3), 469–493. https://doi.org/10.1007/s10551-013-2033-3

Nachira, F., Nicolai, A., Dini, P., Le, L. M., & Leon, L. R. (2007). *Digital business ecosystems, growth macro economy micro economy innovation inclusion efficiency opportunities social science socio-cultural layered infrastructure-adapts to regions cultural/economi*.

Peachey, W., Cohen, A., Shin, N., & Fusaro, B. (2018). Challenges and strategies of building and sustaining inter-organizational partnerships in sport for development and peace. *Sport Management Review*, 21(2), 160–175. https://doi.org/10.1016/j.smr.2017.06.002

Rasche, A. (2012). Global policies and local practice : loose and tight couplings in multi-stakeholder initiatives. *Business Ethic Quarterly*, 22(4), 679–708. https://doi.org/10.5840/beq201222444

Richelieu, A., & Webb, A. (2018). A tale of two networks: contrasting sport for development and peace actor-networks. *Journal of Global Sport Management*, 4(4), 1–21. https://doi.org/10.1080/24704067.2018.1477517

Schulenkorf, N. (2017). Managing sport-for-development: Reflections and outlook. *Sport Management Review*, 20(3), 243–251. https://doi.org/10.1016/j.smr.2016.11.003

Senyo, P. K., Liu, K., & Effah, J. (2019). Digital business ecosystem: Literature review and a framework for future research. *International Journal of Information Management*, 47(June2018), 52–64. https://doi.org/10.1016/j.ijinfomgt.2019.01.002

Shriver, T. (2015). *Annual Report, 2015*. 1–23.

Smith, J. A., & Shinebourne, P. (2012). Interpretative phenomenological analysis. In H. Cooper, P. M. Camic, D. L. Long, A. T., . D. Rindskopf, & K. J. Sher (Eds.), *APA handbook of research methods in psychology, vol 2: Research designs: Quantitative, qualitative, neuropsychological, and biological; APA handbook of research methods in psychology, vol 2: Research designs: Quantitative, qualitative, neuropsychological* (pp. 78). American Psychological Association. https://doi.org/http://dx.doi.org.proxy.library.carleton.ca/10.1037/13620-005

Stadtler, L., & Van Wassenhove, L. N. (2016). Coopetition as a paradox: Integrative approaches in a multi-company, cross-sector partnership. *Organization Studies*, 37(5), 655–685. https://doi.org/10.1177/0170840615622066

Stolle, E. P., Frambaugh-Kritzer, C., Freese, A., & Perrson, A. (2018). What makes a critical friend?: Our journey in understanding this complicated term. In D. Garbett & A. Ovens (Eds.), *Pushing boundaries and crossing borders dawn Garbett and Alan Ovens editors self-study of teacher education practices (S-STEP) self-study as a means for researching pedagogy* (pp. 147–154). Creative Commons Attribution 4.0 International License.

Sugden, J. (2010). Critical left-realism and sport interventions in divided societies. *International Review for the Sociology of Sport*, 45(3), 258–272. https://doi.org/10.1177/1012690210374525

Svensson, P. G., Andersson, F. O., Mahoney, T. Q., & Ha, J. P. (2020). Antecedents and outcomes of social innovation: A global study of sport for development and peace organizations. *Sport Management Review*, 23(4), 657–670. https://doi.org/10.1016/j.smr.2019.08.001

Svensson, P. G., & Hambrick, M. E. (2016). "Pick and choose our battles" - Understanding organizational capacity in a sport for development and peace organization. *Sport Management Review*, 19 (2), 120–132. https://doi.org/10.1016/j.smr.2015.02.003

Svensson, P. G., & Hambrick, M. E. (2019). Exploring how external stakeholders shape social innovation in sport for development and peace. *Sport Management Review*, 22(4), 540–552. https://doi.org/10.1016/j.smr.2018.07.002

Svensson, P. G., Hancock, M. G., & Hums, M. A. (2017). Elements of capacity in youth development nonprofits: An exploratory study of urban sport for development and peace organizations. *Voluntas: International Journal of Voluntary and Nonprofit Organizations, 28*(5), 2053–2080. https://doi.org/10.1007/s11266-017-9876-7

Svensson, P. G., & Loat, R. (2019). Bridge-building for social transformation in sport for development and peace. *Journal of Sport Management, 33*(5), 426–439. https://doi.org/10.1123/jsm.2018-0258

Svensson, P. G., & Woods, H. (2017). A systematic overview of sport for development and peace organisations. *Journal of Sport for Development, 5*(9), 36–48.

Thorpe, H. (2016). 'Look at what we can do with all the broken stuff!' Youth agency and sporting creativity in sites of war, conflict and disaster. *Qualitative Research in Sport, Exercise and Health, 8*(5), 554–570. https://doi.org/10.1080/2159676X.2016.1206957

Webb, A., Richelieu, A., & Cloutier, A. (2019). From clipboards to annual reports: Innovations in sport for development fact management. *Managing Sport and Leisure, 24*(6), 400–423. https://doi.org/10.1080/23750472.2019.1684838

Whitley, M. A., & Welty Peachey, J. (2020). Place-based sport for development accelerators: A viable route to sustainable programming? *Managing Sport and Leisure*, 1–10. https://doi.org/10.1080/23750472.2020.1825989

Williams, M. (2000). Interpretivism and generalisation. *Sociology, 34*(2), 209–224. https://doi.org/10.1177/S0038038500000146

Wilson, J., Johnson, H., & Brotherton, M. L. (2017). From social exclusion to supported inclusion: Adults with intellectual disability discuss their lived experiences of a structured social group. *Journal of Applied Research in Intellectual Disabilities, 30*(5), 847–858. https://doi.org/10.1111/jar.12275

Yin, J., & Jamali, D. (2020). Collide or collaborate: the interplay of competing logics and institutional work in cross-sector social partnerships. *Journal of Business Ethics, 169*(4), 673–694. https://doi.org/10.1007/s10551-020-04548-8

Zhang, J., Jiang, Y., Shabbir, R., & Du, M. (2015). Building industrial brand equity by leveraging firm capabilities and co-creating value with customers. *Industrial Marketing Management, 51*, 47–58. https://doi.org/10.1016/j.indmarman.2015.05.016

Does team identification of satellite fans influence brand-related sponsorship outcomes? What we learned from Manchester United supporters in Malaysia

Charitomeni Tsordia, Artemisia Apostolopoulou and Dimitra Papadimitriou

ABSTRACT
The aim of the research was to explore how satellite fans identification with their favorite foreign team influences sponsorship outcomes. Manchester United and Adidas agreement was examined and a sample of 284 satellite fans from Malaysia was collected using an online survey. The findings provided evidence for the effect of team identification on sponsor-sponsee perceived fit, of perceived fit on sponsor's products perceived brand quality (PBQ) and on word of mouth (WOM), and of PBQ on WOM. Although the direct effect between team identification with PBQ and with WOM was not significant, the results uncovered a full mediating effect of perceived fit in both relationships. The same held true for PBQ on the relationship between team identification and WOM, while PBQ exerted a partial mediating effect on the relationship of perceived fit and WOM. This study offers recommendations on how to strengthen sponsors' return on investment on an international level.

Sport sponsorship has long been considered an effective marketing tool for companies aiming to reach desired target markets domestically and internationally (Mullin et al., 2014). Investments in sport sponsorship have grown steadily. Pre-COVID-19 pandemic predictions for global sport sponsorship spending in 2020 were at $48.4 billion, assisted by mega events such as the Olympic Games and the rise of 'eSports' (Christie, 2020). It is reasonable to assume that teams with strong and global followings are more appealing properties for companies looking to increase their market share by tapping into those teams' international fan bases. Fans outside a team's local market have been labeled satellite fans or supporters (Behrens & Uhrich, 2020; Kerr & Emery, 2011; Kerr & Gladden, 2008), distant fans (Pu & James, 2017), or members of a fan nation (Foster & Hyatt, 2008; Osorio & Hyatt, 2018). The term 'satellite fans' will be used throughout this paper to describe our study population. According to Kerr and Gladden (2008, p. 61), satellite fans are 'those fans who, despite lacking a shared geography, have forged an emotional bond with a foreign-based team.' Given the saturation experienced in teams' domestic areas, marketing strategies geared toward establishing a presence in foreign markets and reaching those international consumers have become common amongst the world's most popular sport franchises (Behrens & Uhrich, 2020).

Existing literature on satellite fans has focused on examining why and how these fans become supporters of a foreign team (Bodet et al., 2020; Kerr & Emery, 2011; Pu & James, 2017); the ways in which sport properties can grow their brands globally and cultivate support from international consumers (Bodet & Chanavat, 2010; Foster & Hyatt, 2008; Hinson et al., 2020; Kerr & Gladden, 2008); and the perceptions of local supporters about the team's satellite fans (Behrens & Uhrich, 2020; Rookwood & Chan, 2011). A number of organization-related (e.g. club history and success, star players, brand elements and merchandising) and market-related (e.g. media coverage, family or friends supporting the team, sponsors) factors have been found to be influential in developing the attachment of those satellite fans (Bodet et al., 2020; Kerr & Emery, 2011; Pu & James, 2017). Furthermore, Foster and Hyatt (2008) have proposed that new and existing traditions can be used by teams to build a fan nation consisting of nonlocal fans who 'can come from anywhere' (p. 266) and who, regardless of their physical location, share an 'imagined cohesiveness' (p. 269) with other team supporters.

Satellite fans can benefit sport properties in a variety of ways including their attendance of games held in the team's local market or abroad, consumption of team-related content on traditional and new media platforms, as well as the purchase of team licensed merchandise and other team extensions (Apostolopoulou & Papadimitriou, 2015; MacIntosh et al., 2020). However, a question that has been relatively unexplored to date is whether satellite fans, through their identification with a foreign team, play a role in the success of that team's corporate partnerships outside the team's local market. In other words, does the existence of organized and highly identified team fans in foreign markets increase the return on team sponsors' investment?

Research on sponsorship outcomes focused specifically on satellite fans is lacking, despite the fact that the involvement of those fans with their chosen foreign teams appears to be considerable. To our knowledge, there is one exception. Wang et al. (2012) examined the perceptions and behaviors of Thai fans of Manchester United and found increased purchase intentions for the services of a team sponsor (AIG) driven by those fans' identification with the team. They also found that the relationship between fan identification and purchase intentions was partially mediated by sponsor credibility and attitude toward the sponsor. The goal of the present study is to build on these findings as it explores whether and in what ways the identification of satellite fans in an emerging market with their favorite foreign sport team influences the transfer of positive perceptions and their behavior toward a sponsor of that team. Focusing on supporters of Manchester United, one of the world's most valued franchises, in the emerging market of Malaysia, this research set out to examine: (a) the impact of team identification on perceived sponsor-sponsee fit and on perceived brand quality of the sponsor's products; (b) the way in which perceived fit affects both sponsorship outcomes of perceived brand quality and word of mouth (WOM) as well as how perceived brand quality affects WOM; (c) the mediating effects of perceived fit in the relationships between team identification and perceived brand quality and team identification and WOM; and (d) the mediating effects of perceived brand quality in the relationships between team identification and WOM and perceived fit and WOM. Along with adding to existing literature involving satellite fans, this research can offer insights into the perceived value of team sponsorship agreements beyond a team's domestic market as well as the structuring and evaluation of those partnerships.

Literature review and hypotheses development

The role of team identification in sport sponsorship

Team identification is an important consideration for sponsors when investing in sport sponsorship, and one of the factors for selecting specific investments (Nassis et al., 2012). It refers to the degree at which an individual (fan) feels psychologically linked to a team (Wann & Branscombe, 1993). This behavior can be explained through social identity theory (Tajfel, 1982), which suggests that the individual transcends his or her own personality in order to develop a social identity that is associated with a social group. The social groups that fans elect to be associated with are sport teams. It is believed that individuals form positive evaluations toward members of the groups they have chosen to belong to (Mullen et al., 1992). Following this concept, team identification is perceived to impact fans' response to the sponsors of their favorite team as these sponsors constitute members of their group. These behaviors could also be true for highly identified satellite fans, as Reifurth et al. (2019) found that increased distance is not negatively related to team identification.

Based on cognitive consistency theories (i.e. Heider, 1958), individuals prefer balanced beliefs as the imbalanced may result in negative psychological feelings. Consequently, they tend to ignore inconsistent information and/or give more importance to consistent one. Gwinner and Bennett (2008) have stated that in sport sponsorship settings, highly identified fans may eliminate possible negative associations for resolving inconsistencies with their favorite sport event and thus maintain a perception of fit between events and sponsorship entities. This might also be true for sport teams, where highly identified fans are expected to be more positive when examining the sponsor-sponsee fit since they will try to maintain the favorability they hold towards the sport team and improve their self-identity, as well. This type of adjustment in perceptions is referred to in the literature as in-group favoritism effect (Branscombe & Wann, (1994)).

Indeed, research in this area has provided support for team identification's positive and significant influence on various sponsorship-related outcomes including perceived fit (Gwinner & Bennett, 2008; Tsordia, Papadimitriou, & Parganas, 2018), brand awareness (Lings & Owen, 2007; Madrigal, 2000), and attitude toward sponsors, sponsor patronage and satisfaction with sponsors (Gwinner & Swanson, 2003). These studies have shown that identification with one's favorite team is strong enough to impact perceptions of congruence that team supporters may develop between the sponsor and the sponsee and, at the same time, their attitudes and perceptions towards the sponsors' brands. Moreover, Greenwell et al. (2002) found that team identification was a major predictor of fans' perceptions of the quality regarding facilities and services, while Fisher and Wakefield (1998) results revealed that identification impacted fans' engagement in purchase behaviors that served as expressions of support toward their favorite team.

It is, therefore, expected that, in the sponsorship context, the stronger a fan's identification with a team, the greater the likelihood that she will evaluate the sponsor-sponsee relationship as having high levels of perceived fit and be more favorable overall toward the team's sponsors. The present study aims to extend those findings to satellite fans by examining whether team identification is influential enough to produce brand-related sponsorship outcomes, such as high levels of perceived quality for the sponsor's brand and increased WOM, amongst those consumers. Based on the above, we propose that:

H1a: Team identification has a positive effect on perceived fit between the sponsor and the sponsee for satellite fans.

H1b: Team identification has a positive effect on perceived brand quality of the sponsor's products for satellite fans.

H1c: Team identification has a positive effect on word of mouth for satellite fans.

Perceived fit between the sponsor and the sport property (sponsee)

In order to understand the brand image transfer process, and ultimately how sponsorship can lead to desirable outcomes for the sponsor, researchers have proposed various theoretical frameworks of image transfer including balance theory, classical conditioning and congruence theory (Novais & Arcodia, 2013). Balance theory suggests that people search for a balance in their attitudes and are willing to change attitudes in order to achieve this balance (Dean, 1999). Within the sponsorship context, balance should be achieved in the relationship between the sponsor, the sponsee (event or entity) and the consumer (Heider, 1946). According to the conceptual framework of classical conditioning, 'it is possible to use an established relationship between a stimulus and response to develop a similar response to a different stimulus' (Novais & Arcodia, 2013, p. 311). In team sponsorship, fans who are exposed to one known (i.e. sport team) and one unknown (i.e. sponsor's brand) stimulus will use the relationship they already have with the team to understand the sponsor's brand (unknown stimulus; Speed & Thompson, 2000), a process that leads to a similar response to both stimuli. Congruence or 'perceived fit' are used to describe the strategic match between a sponsor and a sponsee in terms of their mission, target audience and/or values (Becker-Olsen & Hill, 2006). It is one of the most studied concepts in the sport sponsorship literature and it is seen as a necessary condition in order for the image transfer process from the sponsee to the sponsor to be achieved (Speed & Thompson, 2000). In fact, when there is fit between the sponsor and the sponsee, consumers will experience cognitive consistency that generates more positive responses, while the opposite may result in cognitive inconsistency leading to weaker results (Speed & Thompson, 2000).

Perceived fit has been associated with various positive brand-related outcomes of sponsorship, including perceptions about the quality of a sponsor's products (Henseler et al., 2007; Papadimitriou et al., 2016; Tsordia, Papadimitriou, & Apostolopoulou, 2018), attitude toward the sponsor and intentions to purchase the sponsor's products (Zaharia et al., 2016). In addition, Mazodier and Merunka (2012) found that perceived fit between a sponsor and a sport event significantly and positively influenced brand affect (through consumers' attitude toward the sponsorship) and brand trust, and, in turn, both brand affect and brand trust influenced brand loyalty. Furthermore, it has been found that stronger perceptions of self-congruence with a liked brand are connected with higher levels of WOM behaviors (Wallace et al., 2017). Thus, given what we know about the importance of perceived fit for generating benefits for sponsors (Speed & Thompson, 2000), it is reasonable to assume that this variable will significantly and positively affect various brand-related outcomes for satellite fans, as well. Therefore, the following hypotheses will be examined:

H2a: Perceived fit between the sponsor and the sponsee has a positive effect on perceived brand quality of the sponsor's products for satellite fans.

H2b: Perceived fit between the sponsor and the sponsee has a positive effect on word of mouth for satellite fans.

Brand-related sport sponsorship outcomes

The topic of brand-related sponsorship outcomes has consistently gained attention in the literature (e.g. Cornwell et al., 2001; Donlan, 2014; Roy & Cornwell, 2003). The present study focuses on two of those sponsorship outcomes: perceived brand quality and WOM for the sponsor's products. Perceived brand quality reflects the consumer's perceptions of the overall quality of the brand in relation to its intended purposes and depending on the available alternatives (Zeithaml, 1988). Word of mouth refers to 'the act of consumers providing information about goods, services, brands, or companies to other consumers' (Rosario et al., 2016, p. 297).

Many of the studies exploring the impact of sport sponsorship on a sponsor's brand equity have included perceived brand quality as both a dependent and independent variable (Donlan, 2014; Henseler et al., 2007; Papadimitriou et al., 2016; Tsordia, Papadimitriou, & Parganas, 2018). As a dependent variable, perceived brand quality has been shown to be influenced by sponsorship duration, extent of active management involvement in sponsorship development and sponsorship leverage (Cornwell et al., 2001); by the level of sponsorship and perceived fit (Henseler et al., 2007; Papadimitriou et al., 2016); by exposure to sport sponsorship (Donlan, 2014); and by factors such as brand attitude, brand personality, brand awareness and brand associations (Papadimitriou et al., 2016; Tsordia, Papadimitriou, & Parganas, 2018). As an independent variable, perceived brand quality has emerged significant in impacting brand engagement, brand loyalty, intentions and actual purchase of the sponsor's products (Papadimitriou et al., 2016; Tsordia, Papadimitriou, & Apostolopoulou, 2018).

Word of mouth is considered an influential communications and marketing tool and has been tested empirically in numerous studies as a sport sponsorship outcome (Alexandris et al., 2007; Tsiotsou et al., 2009). Those studies have shown that WOM is influenced by purchase intentions, team attachment and perceptions about a sponsor's image (Tsiotsou et al., 2009), as well as beliefs about sponsorship and the centrality dimension of involvement (Alexandris et al., 2007).

Perceived brand quality and WOM have been linked in existing literature (De Matos & Rossi, 2008; Harrison-Walker, 2001; Zeithaml et al., 1996), offering evidence of the potential of perceived brand quality to predict WOM. In Tsordia, Papadimitriou, and Apostolopoulou's (2018) examination of the sponsorship deal between a basketball club and a software company (videogame console), perceived brand quality was found to significantly influence brand loyalty for the sponsor's product. Word of mouth reflected the behavioral aspect of brand loyalty towards the product. It is generally accepted that when consumers evaluate the quality of a service highly, they are more likely to recommend that service (Harrison-Walker, 2001; Zeithaml et al., 1996). This has held true for products, as well (De Matos & Rossi, 2008). Similarly, when consumers perceive a service as being of low quality, they are more likely to express their disappointment and spread negative WOM about the provider of that service (Zeithaml et al., 1996). Consequently, it is believed that the relationship between perceived brand quality and WOM will be strong for satellite fans of the sponsored team. It is expected that:

H3: Perceived brand quality of the sponsor's products has a positive effect on word of mouth for satellite fans.

The mediating roles of perceived fit and perceived brand quality

The effect of team identification on perceived brand quality and WOM for the products of sponsors has not received extensive examination yet. At the same time, perceived fit has emerged as an indispensable factor for an effective sponsorship deal given the potential of congruence to improve consumer referrals (Wallace et al., 2017), as well as perceptions of quality regarding team sponsors (Henseler et al., 2007; Tsordia, Papadimitriou, & Apostolopoulou, 2018). Henseler et al. (2007) explored the moderating role of perceived fit between sponsor and sponsee in the relationship between sport sponsorship and brand equity as perceived by professional sponsorship managers involved in sponsorship deals with football clubs in the Netherlands. Their findings showed that the relationship was stronger when high levels of perceived fit were present. Moreover, Coelho et al. (2019) focused on perceptions of locals and foreigners who attended the 2014 FIFA Fan Fest in Brazil and found that the relationship between the image of the mega-event and the sponsor's brand equity was partially mediated by the perceptions of fit between the event and the sponsor. The extent to which perceived fit might act as a mediator for these relationships when satellite fans are considered is unexplored. Hence, it is proposed that:

H4a: The relationship between team identification and perceived brand quality of the sponsor's products is mediated by perceived fit between the sponsor and the sponsee for satellite fans.

H4b: The relationship between team identification and word of mouth is mediated by perceived fit between the sponsor and the sponsee for satellite fans.

There is also evidence for the significant effect of perceived fit between the sponsor and the sponsee on the perceptions of the sponsor's brand quality in both sport team (Henseler et al., 2007; Tsordia, Papadimitriou, & Apostolopoulou, 2018) and sport event sponsorship contexts (Papadimitriou et al., 2016). In turn, perceived brand quality for the team sponsor's brand has been found to significantly influence WOM as the behavioral aspect of brand loyalty (Tsordia, Papadimitriou, & Apostolopoulou, 2018). However, the extent to which perceived brand quality for the sponsor's brand might act as a mediator for the relationships of team identification and WOM and of perceived fit between the sponsor and the sponsee and WOM, especially when satellite fans are considered, has yet to be examined. Thus, it is expected that:

H4c: The relationship between team identification and word of mouth is mediated by perceived brand quality of the sponsor's products for satellite fans.

H4d: The relationship between perceived fit between the sponsor and the sponsee and word of mouth is mediated by perceived brand quality of the sponsor's products for satellite fans.

Figure 1 depicts the measurement model designed for the purposes of the present research and shows the relationships among all variables of the study. The mediating effects are shown in Figure 2(a–d). Perceived fit was tested as a mediator for the relationships between team identification and perceived brand quality of the sponsor's products (see Figure 2(a)) and team identification and WOM (see Figure 2(b)). In addition, perceived brand quality was tested as a mediator for the relationships between team identification and WOM (see Figure 2(c)) and perceived fit and WOM (see Figure 2(a)). The mediation analysis divides the total variance, which reflects the total effect explained by the predictor (team identification; perceived fit), into a segment independent of the mediating variable (perceived fit; perceived brand quality) showing the direct effect and a segment dependent on the mediating variable (perceived fit; perceived brand quality) showing the indirect effect.

Methodology

Research setting and data collection

The sponsorship between Manchester United Football Club and Adidas was selected as the research setting for this study. In the European football domain, Manchester United is considered the first to have recognized the dynamic of internationalization and global

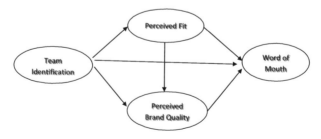

Figure 1. The measurement model.

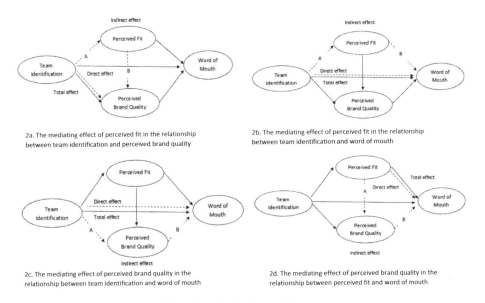

Figure 2. (a–d) The mediating effects hypothesized models.

branding (Hill & Vincent, 2006). Its influence in the global sport marketplace can be seen through the size of the international audience that follows the team: 1.1 billion fans and followers worldwide, a customer relationship management database of more than 36.1 million records globally; record attendance of 109,318 fans in Michigan Stadium in the United States in 2014; over 150 million connections on social media and 9.4 million followers on Chinese social media; and a free global mobile application with monthly active users in over 230 global markets (Manchester United, 2020). Their sponsor Adidas is the second largest sportswear manufacturing company globally with worldwide sales of €23,640 billion in 2019 (Adidas, 2020).

Study participants included Manchester United satellite fans in the developing market of Malaysia. Data were collected in March-May 2017 through an online survey that was uploaded on three Facebook accounts of Manchester United satellite fans in Malaysia. A total of 338 questionnaires were returned. For the purposes of this research, only active consumers of the team sponsor who had bought Adidas products in the past 12 months were considered. As a result, 54 questionnaires were excluded from the database and the final sample consisted of 284 respondents. Literature suggests that running Structural Equation Modeling (SEM) analysis, which is the analysis selected for this study, requires a minimum sample size of 200 respondents (Kline, 2016). That criterion was satisfied and thus the sample size was deemed adequate for analysis.

Instrument and measures

All measures for the four variables used in this research (i.e. team identification, perceived fit between the sponsor and the sponsee, perceived brand quality of the sponsor's products and WOM) were adopted from existing literature. Team identification was measured using four items from Trail and James (2001) and Wann and Branscombe (1993; e.g.

'Being a fan of Manchester United is very important to me'). Perceived fit was measured using three items from Speed and Thompson (2000; e.g. 'There is a logical connection between Manchester United and Adidas'). For perceived brand quality, four items were used from Aaker (1991) and Yoo and Donthu (2001; e.g. 'The products of Adidas have excellent features'). Finally, WOM was measured using three items found in previous studies (Bosnjak et al., 2011; Ferguson et al., 2007; Lee & Xie, 2011; Papadimitriou et al., 2013; Tsiotsou et al., 2009) reflecting the degree to which fans are willing to engage in referral behaviors (e.g. 'I would love to recommend the sponsor's products to my friends'). A 7-point Likert scale (1 = strongly disagree and 7 = strongly agree) was used for all variables.

Data analysis

The analysis of data was conducted using the statistical programs SPSS and SPSS AMOS. First, descriptive statistics (f, %, Means, Standard Deviations) and the correlations of the variables were estimated, followed by a reliability analysis with the Cronbach's α coefficient and a normality test. Then, Confirmatory Factor Analysis (CFA) was run to test the goodness of fit of the measurement model. Various indicators (chi-square χ2; df; x2/df; p-value; CFI; IFI; RMSEA with lower and upper limit; SRMR) were extracted based on the literature (Barrett, 2007; Byrne, 2010; Hu & Bentler, 1999; Kline, 2016; Steiger, 2007). Construct reliability (CR), average variance extracted (AVE) and discriminant validity were additionally tested. Finally, SEM techniques were run to test the research hypotheses using the procedure of bootstrapping, as proposed in existing literature (Arbuckle & Wothke, 1999; Byrne, 2010; West et al., 1995).

Results

Descriptive statistics and correlations

The research sample consisted of 284 respondents, the majority of whom were male (93.7%), 25–34 years of age (58.1%), holding a University degree (49.3%) and employed part or full time (63.4%; see Table 1).

Table 2 displays the means, standard deviations and Spearman's rho correlations between the variables of the study. As shown in Table 2, the sample evaluated all variables highly: team identification (M = 6.63), perceived fit between the sponsor and the sponsee (M = 6.23), perceived brand quality of the sponsor's products (M = 6.34) and WOM (M = 6.07). Furthermore, all variables were positively and significantly inter-correlated.

Confirmatory factor analysis, reliability and validity testing

Confirmatory Factor Analysis was conducted to test the fit of the measurement model and SEM was run to explore the relationships among the variables of the model. Results indicated goodness of fit for the measurement and the structural models (see goodness of fit indices in Tables 3 and 4, respectively). All indicators satisfied the criteria proposed by the literature (Barrett, 2007; Byrne, 2010; Hu & Bentler, 1999; Kline, 2016; Steiger, 2007). The Cronbach's α rates indicated high reliability for all constructs as they ranged from .81 to .95, greater than the recommended threshold of .70 (Nunnally & Bernstein, 1994). Composite reliability,

Table 1. Demographic profile of the sample.

	Variables	F	%
Gender	Male	266	93.7
	Female	18	6.3
	Total	284	100.0
Age	18–24	58	20.4
	25–34	165	58.1
	35–45	55	19.4
	46+	6	2.1
	Total	284	100.0
Educational level	Secondary school	57	20.1
	<4 years education	38	13.4
	University degree	140	49.3
	Post graduate studies	49	17.3
	Total	284	100.0
Employment status	Unemployed	6	2.1
	Student	44	15.5
	Full- or part-time employee	180	63.4
	Self-employed	43	15.1
	Other	11	3.9
	Total	284	100.0

Table 2. Means, standard deviations and correlations.

	M	SD	1	2	3
1. Team identification	6.63	.81	1		
2. Perceived fit	6.23	1.01	.363*	1	
3. Perceived brand quality	6.34	.93	.394*	.592*	1
4. Word of mouth	6.07	1.22	.330*	.619*	.644*

7-point Likert scale, 1 = strongly disagree and 7 = strongly agree, *p < .01,
M = Mean, SD = Standard Deviation.

convergent and discriminant validity were also verified. In particular, CR rates were all above .86 and AVE rates for estimating convergent validity were all above .68. The recommended threshold for CR rates is greater than .70 and for AVE rates it is greater than .50 (Hair et al., 2010; Malhotra & Dash, 2011). Discriminant validity was verified as the squared multiple correlations for each two constructs were lower from the AVE values for each construct (Fornell & Larcker, 1981). Table 3 shows the goodness of fit indices, factor loadings for each item and CR, AVE and Cronbach's *a* rates for all variables included in the model.

Structural model and hypotheses testing

Prior to the analysis, the data set was tested for normality. The results indicated that the three items that comprised the variable of team identification did not satisfy the assumption of normality as their values exceed literature suggestions for univariate skewness (± 3) and kurtosis (±10) (Kline, 2016). The univariate skewness values for the three items were −3,299, −3,361 and −3,520 and the kurtosis values were 12,913, 13,145 and 14,364. In addition, the fact that the data are not normally distributed was indicated by the Mardia's (1970/1974) normalized estimate of multivariate kurtosis rate, which was 178,336 and exceeded the threshold of 5 suggested by Bentler (2005). For this reason, SEM analysis was run to test the research hypotheses using bootstrapping, a method that does not rely on normal distribution and relevant restrictions and, as such, is suggested by the literature for handling non normal data (Byrne, 2010; West et al., 1995).

Table 3. Measures, goodness of fit indices, factor loadings, composite reliability, average variance extracted and Cronbach's *a*.

Constructs	Factor loadings	CR	AVE	*a*
Team identification		.87	.68	.86
(1) I consider myself to be a 'real' fan of the x team	.80			
(1) I would experience a loss if I had to stop being a fan of the x team	Deleted			
(1) Being a fan of x team is very important to me	.90			
(1) During the season, I follow the x team closely on the TV or the internet	.78			
Perceived fit between the sponsor and the team		.86	.68	.81
(1) There is a logical connection between x team and the sponsor	.91			
(1) The image of x team and the image of the sponsor are similar	.61			
(1) The sponsor and the x team fit together well	.92			
Perceived brand quality		.95	.84	.95
1. The quality of the sponsor's products is extremely high	.93			
2. The products of the sponsor have consistent quality	.95			
3. The products of the sponsor have excellent features	.89			
4. The products of the sponsor are very reliable	.89			
Word of mouth		.95	.85	.94
(1) I would love to recommend the sponsor's products to my friends	.95			
(1) I would love to say positive things about the sponsor's products to other people	.96			
(1) I always love to encourage my friends to buy the sponsor's products	.87			

Goodness of fit indices: chi-square χ^2 = 93.995, df = 59, χ^2/df = 1.593; p < .003; CFI = .99; IFI = .99; RMSEA = .046 with lower limit .027, upper limit .063, SRMR = .031
CR = Composite Reliability, AVE = Average Variance Extracted, *a* = Cronbach's Alpha Coefficient.

Table 4. Standardized loadings and variance explained.

Paths	Standardized loadings				Hypotheses
H1a: Team identification → Perceived fit	.66***				Supported
H1b: Team identification → Perceived brand quality	ns				Rejected
H1c: Team identification → Word of mouth	ns				
H2a: Perceived fit → Perceived brand quality	.75***				Supported
H2b: Perceived fit → Word of mouth	.64***				Supported
H3: Perceived brand quality → Word of mouth	.25**				Supported
	IE	DE	TE	MED	
H4(a): Team identification → Perceived fit → Perceived brand quality	.50**	ns	.60**	Full	Supported
H4(b): Team identification → Perceived fit → Word of mouth	.58**	ns	.50**	Full	Supported
H4(c): Team identification → Perceived brand quality → Word of mouth	.58**	ns	.50**	Full	Supported
H4(d): Perceived fit → Perceived brand quality → Word of mouth	.19*	.64**	.83**	Partial	Supported
Variables	**Variance explained (R²)**				
Perceived fit	44%				
Perceived brand quality	68%				
Word of mouth	65%				

*p < .05, **p < .01, ***p < .001
Goodness of fit indices: chi-square χ^2 = 93.995, df = 59, χ^2/df = 1.593; p < .005; CFI = .99; IFI = .99; RMSEA = .046 with lower limit .027, upper limit .063, SRMR = .031
ns = Not Significant; IE = Indirect Effect; DE = Direct Effect; TE = Total Effect; MED = Mediation.

As shown is Table 4, the model explained a significant portion of the variance of perceived fit (R^2 = 44%), perceived brand quality (R^2 = 68%) and WOM (R^2 = 65%). The effects of team identification on perceived fit (β = .66, p < .001), of perceived fit on perceived brand quality (β = .75, p < .001) and WOM (β = .64, p < .001), and of perceived brand quality on WOM (β = .25, p < .01) were positive and significant (see Figure 3), and thus *H1a*, *H2a*, *H2b* and *H3* were supported. Conversely, team identification did not significantly influence perceived brand quality or WOM, leading to the rejection of *H1b* and *H1c*. Regarding the mediating effect of perceived fit on the relationship between team identification and perceived brand quality, the analysis showed a significant indirect

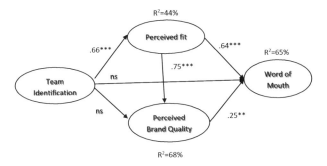

Figure 3. The structural equation model.

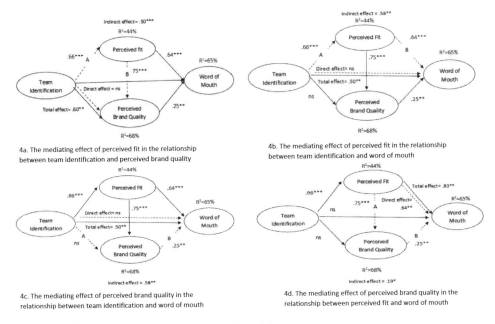

4a. The mediating effect of perceived fit in the relationship between team identification and perceived brand quality

4b. The mediating effect of perceived fit in the relationship between team identification and word of mouth

4c. The mediating effect of perceived brand quality in the relationship between team identification and word of mouth

4d. The mediating effect of perceived brand quality in the relationship between perceived fit and word of mouth

Figure 4. (a–d) The mediating effects structural models.

effect, which indicated the appearance of mediation through perceived fit. However, the direct effect was not significant. These results indicate a full mediation of perceived fit in the relationship between team identification and perceived brand quality and lead to the acceptance of H4a (see Figure 4(a)). The same held true for the mediating effect of both perceived fit between the sponsor and sponsee (see Figure 4(b)) and perceived brand quality (see Figure 4(c)) in the relationship between team identification and WOM, showing the full mediating effect of both variables in the relationship in support of H4b and H4c. Finally, regarding the mediating effect of perceived brand quality on the relationship between perceived fit and WOM, the results indicated significant indirect and direct effects, showing a partial mediating effect of the variable in the relationship (see Figure 4(b)). As such, H4d was supported.

Discussion

This research is one of the first endeavors in the sport sponsorship literature to explore the benefits for a team sponsor (Adidas) from satellite fans of the team (Manchester United Football Club). We have set a conceptual model to explore how team identification mobilizes satellite fans' perceptions of fit between the sponsor and the sponsee and, through those, the extent to which perceived fit affects sponsorship outcomes (i.e. perceived brand quality and WOM). We further investigate the underlying mechanisms of these sponsorship outcomes through the mediating role of perceived fit. Even though there is extensive literature exploring the role of the above variables in understanding how sport sponsorship agreements build benefits for the sponsor in local markets (Donlan, 2014; Gwinner & Bennett, 2008; Henseler et al., 2007; Tsordia, Papadimitriou, & Parganas, 2018), so far there is notable scarcity of investigations of sponsors' benefits associated to satellite fans. Our findings offer evidence in support of the notion that, as teams expand to new markets, brand-related benefits are not confined to the sport properties but also extend to the brands of their sponsors.

The results indicated that team identification of satellite fans directly and positively affects perceived fit between the sponsor and the sponsee (*H1a*), but not perceived brand quality of the sponsor (*H1b*) or WOM (*H1c*). The first part of this finding is consistent with evidence presented by Tsordia, Papadimitriou, and Parganas (2018), suggesting that highly identified fans develop stronger perceptions about the sponsor-sponsee fit; and this appears to be true for satellite fans, as well. We consider this finding an original theoretical contribution of the present study. With respect to the second finding, this study showed that team identification did not have a direct significant impact on how satellite fans evaluated the quality of the sponsor's products. This suggests that satellite fans who are highly attached to a particular foreign team do not automatically form positive perceptions for the team's sponsors. This appears to be a departure from previous research that has established links between satellite fans' team identification and their attitudes toward the sponsors of the team, specifically sponsors' credibility and consumption intentions (Wang et al., 2012). Additional research is needed with samples of satellite fans to further examine this particular relationship.

Although team identification did not directly influence perceived brand quality of the sponsor's products and WOM, these relationships were mediated by perceived fit (*H4a* and *H4b*). Our results show that high team identification was positively related to high levels of perceived fit, which, in turn, had a positive effect on how satellite fans evaluated the quality of the sponsor and on the extent to which they provided positive referrals to friends regarding the sponsor's brand. On the basis of the meaning transfer model (McCracken, 1989), the construct of fit between the sponsor and the sport brand is an important one for explaining the transfer of image-oriented benefits in the context of sponsorship. Moreover, this finding is in line with previous results (Papadimitriou et al., 2016; Speed & Thompson, 2000) that confirm propositions that fit is important for driving attitude formations in the event sponsorship context, and extends those results to include satellite fans of a team.

The effects of perceived fit on perceived brand quality of the sponsor (*H2a*) and on WOM (*H2b*) were significant for satellite fans and in accordance with the proposed direction. In other words, the higher the level of satellite fans' perceptions of fit, the stronger the benefits to the sponsor in terms of those fans viewing their products as having high quality and being willing to spread positive recommendations for the sponsor. The role of functional or image-based fit in building attitudes toward the sponsor is established in the literature involving local fan samples (Gwinner & Bennett, 2008), but not satellite fans. Given that this is the first study that tests these sponsorship outcomes with satellite fans, the results are not readily comparable with previous studies. However, similar to our research, Wang et al. (2012) have underscored the role of satellite fans' team identification in forming positive attitudes toward team sponsors and driving purchase intentions.

Finally, the relationship between satellite fans' perceived brand quality for the sponsor and WOM was positive and statistically significant (H3). This finding is in accordance with earlier studies (De Matos & Rossi, 2008; Harrison-Walker, 2001) that have established the link between perceived brand quality and positive WOM for companies, including affiliated sponsors of professional teams (Tsordia, Papadimitriou, & Parganas, 2018). In addition, while team identification did not emerge as a strong influencer of satellite fans' WOM, perceived brand quality exerted a significant mediating effect on the relationship (H4c) showing that highly identified satellite fans are significantly more eager to convey positive WOM when they hold positive perceptions towards the sponsor's brand quality. Furthermore, and according to the results of our analysis, perceived brand quality strengthened the already strong relationship between perceived fit and WOM (H4d), indicating that it can also influence satellite fans who perceive high fit between the sponsor and the sponsee to provide referrals for the sponsor's brand. Therefore, our results support the position that a well-built brand model for team sponsors involving satellite fans of that team should include the variable of perceived brand quality.

Practical implications

Looking at the results of this study, there are a number of recommendations for sponsorship executives of both teams and sponsors that can increase their leverage with satellite fans. It all starts with being successful in strengthening fans' psychological connection and identification with a team that is located thousands of miles away, and finding ways to incorporate team sponsors in those efforts. Teams should continue their investment in marketing and community outreach initiatives in foreign markets, including offering opportunities to satellite fans to experience the team's core product in person. Initiatives could include playing games and hosting other special events overseas, broadcasting their events via local media outlets, customizing content and delivery on their digital platforms to fit the language and tastes of their satellite fans, and establishing a presence in other countries through ongoing community relations programs. In all those efforts, star power should be front and center, with team players and personnel interacting directly with their satellite fans either in person or virtually through fan clubs, online fan communities and popular social media platforms. This study has shown that being successful in increasing identification levels of satellite fans can be beneficial not only for the team but also for their sponsors, given that perceived fit between the sponsor and the sponsee was positively impacted by team identification and, in turn, perceived fit positively influenced perceptions about the quality of sponsors' products as well as willingness to recommend those products to others.

Our research also revealed that the effect of team identification on sponsors' perceived brand quality and on satellite fans' WOM for the sponsor's brand in both cases was mediated by perceived fit. This suggests that achieving favorable perceptions about the quality of the sponsor's products among satellite fans depends on how well the congruence of the two brands (i.e. sponsor and sponsee) is communicated to fans. This is also important for sponsors who seek to increase the willingness of satellite fans to make positive referrals for their brand to others. It would be strategic for teams to find ways to promote their relationships with their sponsors through traditional and new media outlets and to highlight the quality of the sponsors' products and services. Satellite fans' perceptions of quality also emerged significant in mediating the relationships of team identification and perceived fit with WOM. Sponsors should consistently communicate information about the quality of their brands, including unique attributes and benefits, and design strategies to allow them to engage with both local and nonlocal fans of the teams they sponsor. Fan contests, player appearances, hospitality and special events delivered face-to-face or via digital media platforms are just a few examples of activation that could extend to satellite fans.

Limitations and further research

In closing, there are a few limitations associated with this project that need to be acknowledged and taken into consideration while assessing our results. One such limitation is the fact that the research sample included satellite fans of only one professional football club (Manchester United) from only one country (Malaysia). This means that generalizing the findings of this study to satellite fans of other countries and other teams or even other sports should be done with caution. Future studies are needed with satellite fans from a number of countries in order to gain a more complete understanding of how those fans behave toward the sponsors of a team that is based in a foreign country. Secondly, there was only one sponsor from the sporting goods industry examined in this research. Testing sponsorship outcomes for sponsors from different sectors would allow for a more thorough investigation into the relationships of relevant sponsorship constructs as they pertain to satellite fans.

The third limitation relates to the conceptual model tested in the present study. Consistent with established sponsorship literature, this study set out to explore the role of team identification and perceived fit in strengthening the perceived quality of the sponsor's products and WOM behavior for the sponsor. Besides those outcome variables, other indicators for sponsorship effectiveness that could be included in a future study are purchase intentions and actual purchase behavior. It is reasonable to assume that companies are not only interested in favorable attitudes and consumer intentions when signing sponsorship agreements, but also seek to generate new sales and grow their market share and revenues in return for those investments.

Acknowledgments

The authors wish to thank Bryan Nickson Anak Lomas for assisting with the collection of data for this research.

Disclosure statement

No potential conflict of interest was reported by the author(s).

References

Aaker, D. A. (1991). *Managing brand equity*. The Free Press.
Adidas. (2020). *Adidas at a glance*. https://www.adidas-group.com/en/group/profile/
Alexandris, K., Tsaousi, E., & James, J. (2007). Predicting sponsorship outcomes from attitudinal constructs: The case of a professional basketball event. *Sport Marketing Quarterly, 16* (3), 13–139 https://fitpublishing.com/content/predicting-sponsorship-outcomes-attitudinal-constructs-case-professional-basketball-event-pp.
Apostolopoulou, A., & Papadimitriou, D. (2015). The global sport industry. In J. A. Gillentine & R. B. Crow (Eds.), *Foundations of sport management* (3rd ed., pp. 261–286). Fitness Information Technology.
Arbuckle, J., & Wothke, W. (1999). *AMOS 4 user's reference guide*. Smallwaters Co.
Barrett, P. (2007). Structural equation modelling: Adjudging model fit. *Personality and Individual Differences, 42*(5), 815–824. https://doi.org/10.1016/j.paid.2006.09.018
Becker-Olsen, K. L., & Hill, R. P. (2006). The impact of sponsor fit on brand equity: The case of nonprofit service providers. *Journal of Service Research, 9*(1), 73–83. https://doi.org/10.1177/1094670506289532
Behrens, A., & Uhrich, S. (2020). Uniting a sport teams' global fan community: Prototypical behavior of satellite fans enhances local fans' attitudes and perceptions of groupness. *European Sport Management Quarterly, 20*(5), 598–617. https://doi.org/10.1080/16184742.2019.1643384
Bentler, P.M. (2005) *EQS 6 structural equations program manual*. (Encino, CA: Multivariate Software.)
Bodet, G., & Chanavat, N. (2010). Building global football brand equity: Lessons from the Chinese market. *Asia Pacific Journal of Marketing and Logistics, 22*(1), 55–66. https://doi.org/10.1108/13555851011013155
Bodet, G., Geng, H., Chanavat, N., & Wang, C. (2020). Sport brands' attraction factors and international fans. *Sport, Business and Management: An International Journal, 10*(2), 147–167. https://doi.org/10.1108/SBM-12-2018-0107
Bosnjak, M., Sirgy, J. M., Hellriegel, S., & Maurer, O. (2011). Positivist destination loyalty judgments: Developing and testing a comprehensive congruity model. *Journal of Travel Research, 50*(5), 496–508. https://doi.org/10.1177/0047287510379159
Branscombe, N., and Wann, D. (1994) Collective self-esteem consequences of outgroup derogation when a valued social identity is on trial. *European Journal of Social Psychology*, 24, 641–657.
Byrne, B. M. (2010). *Structural equation modeling with AMOS: Basic concepts, applications, and programming* (2nd ed.). Routledge/Taylor & Francis.
Christie, D. (2020). *Sports sponsorship spend to increase the most in a decade, report says* Marketing Dive . https://www.marketingdive.com/news/sports-sponsorship-spend-to-increase-the-most-in-a-decade-report-says/571295/
Coelho, M. G. R., de Amorim, J. G. B., & Almeida, V. M. C. (2019). Sports mega-event sponsorship: The impact of FIFA reputation and world cup image on sponsor brand equity. *BAR, Brazilian Administration Review, 16*(1), e180071. https://doi.org/10.1590/1807-7692bar2019180071
Cornwell, T. B., Roy, D. P., & Steinard, E. A. (2001). Exploring managers' perceptions of the impact of sponsorship on brand equity. *Journal of Advertising, 30*(2), 41–51. https://doi.org/10.1080/00913367.2001.10673636
De Matos, C. A., & Rossi, C. A. V. (2008). Word-of-mouth communications in marketing: A meta-analytic review of the antecedents and moderators. *Journal of the Academy of Marketing Science, 36*(4), 578–596. https://doi.org/10.1007/s11747-008-0121-1
Dean, D. H. (1999). Brand endorsement, popularity and event sponsorship as advertising cues affecting consumer prepurchase attitudes. *Journal of Advertising, 28*(3), 1–12. https://doi.org/10.1080/00913367.1999.10673585

Donlan, L. (2014). An empirical assessment of factors affecting the brand-building effectiveness of sponsorship. *Sport, Business and Management: An International Journal*, 4(1), 6–25. https://doi.org/10.1108/SBM-09-2011-0075

Ferguson, J. R., Paulin, M., & Leiriao, E. (2007). Loyalty and positive word-of-mouth. *Health Marketing Quarterly*, 23(3), 59–77. https://doi.org/10.1080/07359680802086174

Fisher, R. J., & Wakefield, K. (1998). Factors leading to group identification: A field study of winners and losers. *Psychology & Marketing*, 15(1), 23–40. https://doi.org/10.1002/(SICI)1520-6793(199801)15:1<23::AID-MAR3>3.0.CO;2-P

Fornell, C., & Larcker, D. F. (1981). Evaluating structural equation models with unobservable variables and measurement error. *Journal of Marketing Research*, 18(1), 39–50. https://doi.org/10.1177/002224378101800104

Foster, W. M., & Hyatt, C. G. (2008). Inventing team tradition: A conceptual model for the strategic development of fan nations. *European Sport Management Quarterly*, 8(3), 265–287. https://doi.org/10.1080/16184740802224183

Greenwell, C. T., Fink, J. S., & Pastore, D. L. (2002). Perceptions of the service experience: Using demographic and psychographic variables to identify customer segments. *Sport Marketing Quarterly*, 11 (4), 233–241 https://fitpublishing.com/content/perceptions-service-experience-using-demographic-and-psychographic-variables-identify.

Gwinner, K., & Bennett, G. (2008). The impact of brand cohesiveness and sport identification on brand fit in a sponsorship context. *Journal of Sport Management*, 22(4), 410–426. https://doi.org/10.1123/jsm.22.4.410

Gwinner, K., & Swanson, S. R. (2003). A model of fan identification: Antecedents and sponsorship outcomes. *Journal of Services Marketing*, 17(3), 275–294. https://doi.org/10.1108/08876040310474828

Hair, J. F., Black, B., Babin, J. B., & Anderson, E. R. (2010). *Multivariate data analysis* (7th Global ed.). Pearson Education.

Harrison-Walker, L. J. (2001). The measurement of word-of-mouth communication and an investigation of service quality and customer commitment as potential antecedents. *Journal of Service Research*, 4(1), 60–75. https://doi.org/10.1177/109467050141006

Heider, F. 1958 *The psychology of interpersonal relations*. (New York: Wiley)

Heider, F. (1946). Attitudes and cognitive organization. *Journal of Psychology*, 21(1), 107–112. https://doi.org/10.1080/00223980.1946.9917275

Henseler, J., Wilson, B., Gotz, O., & Hautvast, C. (2007). Investigating the moderating role of fit on sports sponsorship and brand equity. *International Journal of Sports Marketing & Sponsorship*, 8(4), 34–42. https://doi.org/10.1108/IJSMS-08-04-2007-B005

Hill, J. S., & Vincent, J. (2006). Globalisation and sports branding: The case of Manchester United. *International Journal of Sports Marketing and Sponsorship*, 7(3), 213–230. https://doi.org/10.1108/IJSMS-07-03-2006-B008

Hinson, R. E., Osabutey, E., Kosiba, J. P., & Asiedu, F. O. (2020). Internationalisation and branding strategy: A case of the English Premier League's success in an emerging market. *Qualitative Market Research: An International Journal*, 23(4), 747–766. https://doi.org/10.1108/QMR-12-2017-0188

Hu, L.-T., & Bentler, P. M. (1999). Cutoff criteria for fit indexes in covariance structure analysis: Conventional criteria versus new alternatives. *Structural Equation Modeling: A Multidisciplinary Journal*, 6(1), 1–55. https://doi.org/10.1080/10705519909540118

Kerr, A. K., & Emery, P. R. (2011). Foreign fandom and the Liverpool FC: A cyber-mediated romance. *Soccer & Society*, 12 (6), 880–896 doi:10.1080/14660970.2011.609686.

Kerr, A. K., & Gladden, J. M. (2008). Extending the understanding of professional team brand equity to the global marketplace. *International Journal of Sport Management and Marketing*, 3(1/2), 58–77. https://doi.org/10.1504/IJSMM.2008.015961

Kline, R. B. (2016). *Principles and practice of structural equation modeling* (4th ed.). Guilford.

Lee, J., & Xie, L. K. (2011). *Cognitive destination image, destination personality and behavioral intentions: An integrated perspective of destination branding* [Paper presentation]. The 16th Graduate Students Research Conference. Amherst, MA: University of Massachusetts.

Lings, I. N., & Owen, K. M. (2007). Buying a sponsor's brand: The role of affective commitment to the sponsored team. *Journal of Marketing Management*, 23(5–6), 483–496. https://doi.org/10.1362/026725707X212784

MacIntosh, E. W., Bravo, G. A., & Li, M. (2020). *International sport management* (2nd ed.). Human Kinetics.

Madrigal, R. (2000). The influence of social alliances with sports teams on intentions to purchase corporate sponsors' products. *Journal of Advertising*, 29(4), 13–24. https://doi.org/10.1080/00913367.2000.10673621

Malhotra, N. K., & Dash, S. (2011). *Marketing research: An applied orientation*. Pearson Publishing.

Manchester United. (2020). *About Manchester United*. https://ir.manutd.com/company-information/about-manchester-united.aspx

Mardia, K.V. (1970) Measures of multivariate skewness and kurtosis with applications. *Biometrika*, 57, 519–530.

Mardia, K.V. (1974). Applications of some measures of multivariate skewness and kurtosis in testing normality and robustness studies. *Sankhya*, B36, 115–128.

Mazodier, M., & Merunka, D. (2012). Achieving brand loyalty through sponsorship: The role of fit and self-congruity. *Journal of the Academy of Marketing Science*, 40(6), 807–820. https://doi.org/10.1007/s11747-011-0285-y

McCracken, G. (1989). Who is the celebrity endorser? Cultural foundations of the endorsement process. *Journal of Consumer Research*, 16(3), 310–321. https://doi.org/10.1086/209217

Mullen, B., Brown, R., & Smith, C. (1992). Ingroup bias as a function of salience, relevance, and status: An integration. *European Journal of Social Psychology*, 22(2), 103–122. https://doi.org/10.1002/ejsp.2420220202

Mullin, B. J., Hardy, S., & Sutton, W. A. (2014). *Sport marketing* (4th ed.). Human Kinetics.

Nassis, P., Theodorakis, N., Alexandris, K., Afthinos, Y., & Tsellou, A. (2012). Testing the role of team identification on the relationship between sport involvement and sponsorship outcomes in the context of professional soccer. *International Journal of Sport Management*, 13 (4) , 1–17.

Novais, M. A., & Arcodia, C. (2013). Measuring the effects of event sponsorship: Theoretical frameworks and image transfer models. *Journal of Travel & Tourism Marketing*, 30(4), 308–334. https://doi.org/10.1080/10548408.2013.784149

Nunnally, J. C., & Bernstein, I. H. (1994). *Psychometric theory* (3rd ed.). McGraw-Hill.

Osorio, B., & Hyatt, C. (2018). Nonlocal Portuguese football fans and their love for the "Big Three". In J. J. Zhang & B. G. Pitts, (Eds.), *The global football industry: Marketing perspectives* (pp. 78–100). Routledge.

Papadimitriou, D., Apostolopoulou, A., & Kaplanidou, K. (2013). Destination personality, affective image, and behavioral intentions in domestic urban tourism. *Journal of Travel Research*, 54(3), 302–315. https://doi.org/10.1177/0047287513516389

Papadimitriou, D., Kaplanidou, K., & Papacharalampous, N. (2016). Sport event-sponsor fit and its effects on sponsor purchase intentions: A non-consumer perspective among athletes, volunteers and spectators. *Journal of Business & Industrial Marketing*, 31(2), 247–259. https://doi.org/10.1108/JBIM-09-2014-0187

Pu, H., & James, J. (2017). The distant fan segment: Exploring motives and psychological connection of international National Basketball Association fans. *International Journal of Sports Marketing and Sponsorship*, 18(4), 418–438. https://doi.org/10.1108/IJSMS-05-2016-0022

Reifurth, K. R. N., Bernthal, M. J., Ballouli, K., & Collins, D. (2019). Nonlocal fandom: Effects of geographic distance, geographic identity, and local competition on team identification. *Sport Marketing Quarterly*, 28(4), 195–208. https://doi.org/10.32731/SMQ.284.122019.02

Rookwood, J., & Chan, N. (2011). The 39th game: Fan responses to the Premier League's proposal to globalize the English game. *Soccer & Society*, 12(6), 897–913. https://doi.org/10.1080/14660970.2011.609688

Rosario, A. B., Sotgiu, F., De Valck, K., & Bijmolt, T. H. A. (2016). The effect of electronic word of mouth on sales: A meta-analytic review of platform, product, and metric factors. *Journal of Marketing Research*, 53(3), 297–318. https://doi.org/10.1509/jmr.14.0380

Roy, D. P., & Cornwell, B. T. (2003). Brand equity's influence on responses to event sponsorships. *Journal of Product & Brand Management*, *12*(6), 377–393. https://doi.org/10.1108/10610420310498803

Speed, R., & Thompson, P. (2000). Determinants of sports sponsorship response. *Journal of the Academy of Marketing Science*, *28*(2), 226–238. https://doi.org/10.1177/0092070300282004

Steiger, J. H. (2007). Understanding the limitations of global fit assessment in structural equation modeling. *Personality and Individual Differences*, *42*(5), 893–898. https://doi.org/10.1016/j.paid.2006.09.017

Tajfel, H. (1982). Social psychology of intergroup relation. *Annual Review of Psychology*, *33*(1), 1–30. https://doi.org/10.1146/annurev.ps.33.020182.000245

Trail, G. T., & James, J. D. (2001). The motivation scale for sport consumption: Assessment of the scale's psychometric properties. *Journal of Sport Behavior*, *24* (1), 108–127.

Tsiotsou, R., Alexandris, K., & Runyan, R. C. (2009). Delineating the outcomes of sponsorship. *International Journal of Retail & Distribution Management*, *37*(4), 358–369. https://doi.org/10.1108/09590550910948583

Tsordia, C., Papadimitriou, D., & Apostolopoulou, A. (2018). Building a sponsor's equity through brand personality: Perceptions of fans and rivals. *Sport, Business and Management: An International Journal*, *8*(5), 454–468. https://doi.org/10.1108/SBM-09-2017-0050

Tsordia, C., Papadimitriou, D., & Parganas, P. (2018). The influence of sport sponsorship on brand equity and purchase behavior. *Journal of Strategic Marketing*, *26*(1), 85–105. https://doi.org/10.1080/0965254X.2017.1374299

Wallace, E., Buil, I., & de Chernatony, L. (2017). Consumers' self-congruence with a "Liked" brand: Cognitive network influence and brand outcomes. *European Journal of Marketing*, *5*(2), 367–390. https://doi.org/10.1108/EJM-07-2015-0442

Wang, M. C. H., Jain, M., Cheng, J. M. S., & Aung, G. K. M. (2012). The purchasing impact of fan identification and sports sponsorship. *Marketing Intelligence & Planning*, *30*(5), 553–566. https://doi.org/10.1108/02634501211251052

Wann, D. L., & Branscombe, N. R. (1993). Sports fans: Measuring degree of identification with their teams. *International Journal of Sport Psychology*, *24* (1), 1–17.

West, S. G., Finch, J. F., & Curran, P. J. (1995). Structural equation models with nonnormal variables: Problems and remedies. In R. H. Hoyle (Ed.), *Structural equation modeling: Concepts, issues, and applications* (pp. 56–75). Sage.

Yoo, B., & Donthu, N. (2001). Developing and validating a multidimensional consumer-based brand equity scale. *Journal of Business Research*, *52*(1), 1–14. https://doi.org/10.1016/S0148-2963(99)00098-3

Zaharia, N., Biscaia, R., Gray, D., & Stotlar, D. (2016). No more "good" intentions: Purchase behaviors in sponsorship. *Journal of Sport Management*, *30*(2), 162–175. https://doi.org/10.1123/jsm.2015-0347

Zeithaml, V. A., Berry, L. L., & Parasuraman, A. (1996). The behavioral consequences of service quality. *Journal of Marketing*, *60*(2), 31–47. https://doi.org/10.1177/002224299606000203

Zeithaml, V. A. (1988). Consumer perceptions of price, quality, and value: A means-end model and synthesis of evidence. *Journal of Marketing*, *52*(3), 2–22. https://doi.org/10.1177/002224298805200302

Index

Note: Figures are indicated by *italics*. Tables are indicated by **bold**. Endnotes are indicated by the page number followed by 'n' and the endnote number e.g., 20n1 refers to endnote 1 on page 20.

Aaker, D. A. 2, 98
Actor-Network Theory (ANT) 78
Adams, J. 60, 62
Algesheimer, R. 30
AMOS 20.0 software 32
Anderson, J. R. 12
Ansoff, H. I. 11
Apostolopoulou, A. 95
Australian-based consumers 19–20
Australian Football League Women's (AFLW) competition 10
average numbers **65**
average variance extracted (AVE) 30, 98

Bagozzi, R. P. 28
balance theory 93
Barça Foundation Museum 40, 45–7
Bennett, G. 92
Bentler, P. M. 99
Bertschy, M. 45
Bourdieu, P. 66
Boyle, B. A. 27
brand architecture 12
brand associations 2, 12–13, **13**
brand awareness 2
brand equity 2; CSR 26–7; online community identification 28
brand identity 2
brand loyalty 2
Branscombe, N. R. 30
Braun, V. 78
Broadcasters' Audience Research Board (BARB) 57
broadcasting channel (BBC) 63
broadcasts selection 60, **61**

Chambers, T. 67
Chang, M. J. 25
codebook variables 62, **64**
Coelho, M. G. R. 95
commercial breaks 59

composite reliability (CR) 31
confirmatory factor analysis (CFA) **32**, 98–9
congruence/perceived fit 93
construct reliability 98
Consumer Attitudes toward Responsible Entities in Sport (CARES) scale 30
convergent validity **32**
corporate social responsibility (CSR): and brand equity 26–7; brand management 24; consumers' supporting behavioural intentions 24; fan-to-fan relationships 25; measurement model 30–1, **31–2**; online-based communication techniques 25; professional sport teams 35; and team identification 25–7; *see also* online community identification
Creswell, J. W. 16

Debord, G. 39, 41; gamification 41–2; society of spectacles 41; sportainment and Schumpeter's creative destruction 43–5, *43*
Delia, E. B. 11
descriptive statistics and correlations 98, **99**
Dholakia, U. M. 28
discriminant validity 31, **32**, 98
Diversity and Inclusion 16, 18, 19
Donthu, N. 98
Doyle, J. P. 4

education/entertainment technology 47
Eisenhardt, K. M. 45, 46, 78; method **56**

Fan Lifetime Value (FLV) 42
Fatma, While 28–9
FC Barcelona (FCB) 40, 48, 84
Fisher, R. J. 92
formality of connections 81
Foster, W. M. 91
frequency of connections 81
Fulmer, R. M. 1–2
Funding Limitations 16, 18, 19

Gabriel, Y. 39, 41
gamification 39–42
Giulianotti, R. 59
Gladden, J. M. 90
Graham, A. 60, 62
Greenwell, C. T. 92
Gwinner, K. 92

Heere, B. 30
Henseler, J. 95
Hur, W. M. 34
Hyatt, C. G. 91
hypotheses testing 99–101

International Olympics Committee 84
International Paralympic Committee 84
interpretive phenomenological analysis (IPA) 78
inter-rater reliability (IRR) 62
Ireland, R. 5

Jang, H. 28
Jin, B. 28, 34

Katz, M. 26
Keller, K. L. 2
Kent, A. 26
Kenyon, J. A. 4
Kerr, A. K. 90
Kim, S. 4

Lack of Coverage 16, 18, 19
Latour, B. 46

Madrid, Atletico 10
Magnusson, P. 27
Major Soccer League (MLS) 9
Manchester United supporters 90
Martínez, P. 34
Mazodier, M. 93–4
measurement model *96*
mediating effects hypothesized models *97*
mediating effects structural models *101*
mega-event sponsors 58–9
Merunka, D. 93–4
Microsoft Excel 2016 62
Morrison, K. A. 25, 33
multi-stakeholder partnerships: description 74; SOC 74
Mumcu, C. 11
museum staging 47

Naraine, M. L. 42
National Collegiate Athletic Association 84
National Rugby League Women (NRLW) 10
National Women's Soccer League (NWSL) 9
Netball (Super Netball) 10
New Opportunities 16, 18, 19
Nishiyama, N. 34
non-communicable diseases (NCDs) 58

Ofcom report 66
online community identification 26; and brand equity 28; perceived CSR 28–9, *29*
Orr, K. 5

Paché, G. 41
Papadimitriou, D. 95, 102
Parent, M. M. 43
Parganas, P. 102
partnership equity: and brand value 82; corporate brands 82; and individual value 82–4
partnership management matrix 80–2, *81*
Peachey, W. 75
perceived brand quality 2, 95–6
perceived fit 93–4
Polo-Peña, A. I. 42
Popp, B. 28
Pracejus, J. W. 58
procedure and inter-rater reliability 62
Purves, R. I. 59, 60, 62

quantitative methods 20

Reifurth, K. R. N. 92
reliability and validity testing 98–9
Richelieu, A. 4, 43
Robertson, R. 59
Role Models 16, 18, 19
Roper, S. 42
Ross, S. D. 46
Rugby Union (Super W) 10

Sassi, F. 67
satellite fans 90–1
Singh, A. 28–9
Soccer (W-League) 10
social identity-brand equity (SIBE) model 27
South Korean Baseball Organisation (KBO) 29–30
Special Olympics Canada (SOC) 74, 76–7
sponsor and sport property (sponsee) 93–4
sportainment 40; and Schumpeter's creative destruction 43–5
sport brands management 3, 10–11
sport for development (SFD): analysis 78; challenges 75; complexity of 75–6; description 74; design 77; and peace 40, 46, 50; recruitment and data collection 77–8; research objectives and questions 77; rigor 78–9; Special Olympics (SO) Canada 76–7; transnational partnerships 75
Sport Spectator Identification Scale 30
sport sponsorship 58–9; brand-related 94–5; team identification 92–3
SPSS version 24 62
stakeholders 3; stakeholder overlap 3
standard deviations (SD) **65**
standard errors of means (SE) **65**

standardised factor loading 30
strategic brand management: in sport 3–4; through sport 4–6
Strategic Sportainment Mix *49*
structural equation model 99–101, *101*

Tang, Y. Y. 27, 34
team identification 25–6; and brand equity 27; sport sponsorship 92–3
tech-celeration 40
Thorpe, A. S. 42
traditional and digital media proliferation 3
traditional sport-related entertainment 47
Tsordia, C. 6, 95, 102

Uhm, J. P. 45
Underwood, R. 27, 35
unhealthy brands: broadcast sport 59; marketing references 60
unique decision pathways 79–80
United Nations (UN) sustainable development goals 46

Verma, P. 28–9

Wakefield, K. 92
Walker, M. 26, 30
Wang, M. C. H. 27, 34, 91, 103
Wann, D. L. 30
Watkins, B. A. 27, 30, 34
Wear, H. 27
Webb, A. 4, 5
Weick, K. E. 45
Women's Big Bash League (WBBL) 10
women's sport brands 11–12
women's sport teams: measurement 14; respondent demographics and favourite team selections 14, **15**; sample and data collection 14; Sydney Roosters 13–14
Woo, H. 28, 34
Woratschek, H. 28
word of mouth (WOM) 91–2, 94–5

Yan, G. 42
Yoo, B. 98
Yoshida, M. 26

Taylor & Francis eBooks

www.taylorfrancis.com

A single destination for eBooks from Taylor & Francis with increased functionality and an improved user experience to meet the needs of our customers.

90,000+ eBooks of award-winning academic content in Humanities, Social Science, Science, Technology, Engineering, and Medical written by a global network of editors and authors.

TAYLOR & FRANCIS EBOOKS OFFERS:

- A streamlined experience for our library customers
- A single point of discovery for all of our eBook content
- Improved search and discovery of content at both book and chapter level

REQUEST A FREE TRIAL
support@taylorfrancis.com